Walk or

396   528   741   963   285

Walk on Water

417   639   852   174

Dr. Leonard G. Horowitz

Tetrahedron Publishing Group
Sandpoint, Idaho

OTHER BOOKS BY DR. LEN HOROWITZ

Healing Codes for the Biological Apocalypse

Death in the Air: Globalism, Terrorism & Toxic Warfare

Healing Celebrations: Miraculous Recoveries Through Ancient Scripture, Natural Medicine & Modern Science

Emerging Viruses: AIDS & Ebola—Nature, Accident or Intentional?

DNA: Pirates of the Sacred Spiral

Evil hates truth most!
You've heard it said, 'The truth shall set you free.'
There's no *if*s, *and*s or *but*s about it.
The greatest truths are *optimally* freeing. . . .

This contribution provides gigantic truths,
for which all credit must be heavenly directed.

May these truths be an ongoing force for divine spiritual
strengthening and planet-wide healing.

Tetrahedron, LLC

Health Science Communications for People Around the World

Cover designed by Len Horowitz
Manufactured in the United States of America

10 9 8 7 6 5 4 3 2 1

Library of Congress Cataloging Preassigned
Horowitz, Leonard G.
 Walk on Water
 p.   cm.
 Includes bibliographical references.
 1. Popular Works;   2. Religion
  —Health science—Genetics   —Intelligent design—Creationism
  —Alternative medicine—Physics
  —Energy medicine—Mathematics
  —Water science—Bioenergetics
 3. Health Education   4. Spiritual Healing
 5. Judeo-Christian Theology

Card Number: Pending
Additional cataloging data pending.

ISBN: 0-923550-37-2

Additional copies of this book are available for bulk purchases.
For more information, please contact:
Tetrahedron, LLC • Suite 147, 206 North 4th Avenue • Sandpoint, Idaho 83864,
1-888-508-4787; Fax: 808-965-2002, E-mail: tetra@tetrahedron.org,
URL web site: http://www.tetrahedron.org

First printing

Contents

Foreword

by Rev. Richard S.C. Kirby, Ph.D.
President and Chaplain, Kepler Academy, Inc.;
Chaplain, World Network of Religious Futurists

The Spirit of Health, like the Path of Healing, is a subject of great importance not only to health professionals but to all human beings and the Kingdoms or realms over which they exercise dominion. There is a natural hunger in the healthy heart, or even the unhealthy heart, for the Path of Healing, which is known in spiritual traditions by many other names such as the Way of Peace, or just *The Way*—for this has in apostolic times the name given to the Christian or Jewish–Christian path before Christianity split from its mother Judaism—or the Way of Salvation, or the Way of the Lord. Thus, for example the first Psalm declares: "How blest is the One who walks in the Way of the Lord," and the acrostic 119th Psalm tells us repeatedly that the Word of the Lord—the Torah, the Pentateuch, the Prophecies, the New Testament—is a lamp or lantern unto our feet.

There is a profound and inalienable connection between holiness—walking in the way of the Lord—and wholeness or wellness or health. Spiritual thinkers, religious philosophers, healing professionals and medical mystics, among many other constituencies which could be listed understand well the deep and inextricable connection between moral or spiritual health on the one hand and physical, mental and even socio-political health on the other. Indeed, Paul Townier, writing in such books as the *Meaning of Persons*, as a medical psychoanalyst and author of *A Doctor's Casebook in the light of the Bible*, reminds us that while psychoanalysis observes that actions contrary to "deep-seated moral ideas" cause mental pain, or anguish and guilt, the Bible simply calls this "sin." However, the Judeo-Christian ethic and morality is not addressed to the guilt or moral error of the individual, but the waywardness of the group, tribe, people or ethnos—and that collective punishment. Isaiah, Jeremiah, Amos, Joel, Hosea and others warn Israel—the people of God—that social or political disorder or unwellness—moral sickness—can only have the gravest consequences, from poverty and illness to exile or annihilation. But the Bible lets God, and hope, have the last word. It offers not condemnation but a new beginning. Repentance earns, not punishment, but a new beginning in a love relationship between the Creator and His holy people in their community.

Moral health and public health go hand in hand. Good government is rewarded with civic wellness, bad government condemns the citizens to collective illness of many kinds, and puts them and their community in danger of the gravest perils threatening their prosperity, their health, their soul's true ideal.

The study of medical ethics and of medical finance has become a veritable industry. Behind and perhaps above it lies the search for absolute truth, absolute goodness—the absolute presence of the Supreme Being, the living and fresh Word of the living God.

Many constituencies share this yearning for the New Word of God relative to the healing sciences, and industries and arts and communities. Philosophers and theologians create their 'theologies of healing,' inspired physicians publish their 'principles of healthy living,' pastors and rabbis declare the need to turn back to God, mystics proclaim subtle laws of subtle 'bodies' health, whistle-blowers disclose the dark and selfish deeds of medical "malefactors of great wealth"—and along comes the brave prophetic voice of Leonard G. Horowitz in his 2006 treatise and call, *Walk on Water*.

Dr. Horowitz, a medical professional mystic and prophet, combines many of these voices into his own single voice of warning, exhortation, information and hope for the infinite healing by the Way of Yahweh, the Way of Christ, the Way of the Divine Lover. In an intimate and personal but deeply reverent and nonetheless scholarly tone, he conveys to the general public urgent truths, and reports divine revelations and their associated "Healing Codes." Dr. Horowitz continually educates us while he inspires and exhorts, and in a wonderful journey connecting spiritual science to healing science, physical science, mathematical science and political science, he shows the Davidian Music in the Key of Life, and points the way for a healing and healers' lifestyle of worship, wellness and civic authenticity. Let us hope that millions will enter his declared Way, his 'perfect step' within the universal symphony; may his earnestness and moral zeal win the heart and mind of the medico-financial world!

Richard S.C. Kirby, Ph.D., M. Div.*

* Dr. Richard Kirby is chairman emeritus of the World Network of Religious Futurists. For more than 25 years he has exquisitely shared his vision for helping religionists and futurists learn from each other's worlds. The author of ten books and many brilliant essays, many of his articles may be freely downloaded from the WNRF website at: http://www.wnrf.org/cms/drrskirby.shtml. His contact address is: drkirby@newgenius.com

Walk on Water

Preface

Is God Home? He is supposed to be living in your Temple. He was when you were born. Did you evict him? Have you been entertaining lesser substitutes—ABC, CBS, NBC, CNN, or FOX? They each say they know what's best for you and what you should or shouldn't do. Can they offer heaven on Earth, or just a pseudo-reality in which you live vicariously through celebrity heros and news bozos. You trust them and they poison you. They don't call it "the rat race" for nothing. Care about freedom? Read this book and get a new life. When you get to the end, you'll have a new beginning. You may even ask God to return home, and serve to make him stay.

This book explains many incredible things. My ears longed to hear, and my eyes sought to see, truths of various kinds, particularly Divine ones. "Seek and ye shall find, ask and you will receive." So an angel came to me and gave me this prologue to wet your appetite for the amazing revelations herein.

To begin this discovery, consider what our living God urged the Churches, Mosques, Synagogues, and Holy Temples of all time to keep in mind and take to heart. It has to do with fools gold versus the real wealth available in the Kingdom of Heaven, which you are supposed to seek first, before wealth or anything else.

Revelation 3 refers to the Church in the gold capital of Sardis—the wealthiest island on ancient trade routes around the time the New Testament story began. Great wealth, especially in gold, is very appealing to most people. This was paradise to many of the wealthiest Hebrew elite. It was the gold gathering Mecca of the old world.

Gold is mentioned from the beginning to the end of the Bible. It always symbolized divinity, or that which is godlike, for people of all theologies. From Genesis 2:11-12, gold was found when Adam arose by the Holy Spirit of Yah's breath. In the rapidly approaching last days of Revelation 21:18, 21, a "remnant" of protected people walk heaven's streets paved with gold as the promised paradise restores the planet. I wonder if you will witness this. I'd love you to. I'm pretty sure I will. At least my training for the event is going pretty well.

Joseph of Aramathea, Yahshua's (Jesus's) Jewish uncle, sailed to Sardis on many occasions to advance his gold trade and merchant marine business. He owned a magnificent fleet of merchant ships that are believed to have sailed the seven seas from the Mediterranean to Asia and the Americas.

By the way, Yahshua means "Yah (God) saves." So with gold symbolic of divinity, it is safe to bet that Joseph invested his gold to help save the rest of his divine royal family following Yahshua's stirring transformation and reappearance.

Centuries later, the Knights Templar and the Roman Catholic Church accumulated the greatest gold. The Templar's took control over the global merchant marine. Our current system of maritime law dates to this era.

Along with gathering massive wealth, and the secreted knowledge from ancient scripture accumulated over the centuries, including the sacred scrolls taken from King Solomon's Temple in Jerusalem, the Templars funded the "Holy Wars" of the world. Eventually, in the fourteenth century, they earned the wrath and execution writ of Pope Clement V allied with King Philip IV of England. Forewarned of their enemies' attack, the Templar knights escaped by sea with their massive fortune. The act established the lore of their disappearance date—Friday, October 13, 1307. These enemies of the Church and Anglican state became known as the world's first pirates. Their skull and bones insignia evolved from the red bloodied cross of Christ.

Now, here's your recommended reading from Revelation 3:2-6; 14-22. It was written as a warning for Templar descendents—our New World Order leaders and architects—and the profiteering industrialists working to advance contemporary agendas. This book petitions the members of this extended royal family who know the truth, and have been increasingly moved to resist *my* relatives' evil temptations. Many brothers and sisters of royalty, like common folks, have walked in truth and increasingly feel Divine conscience forcing their repentance. So, here are the words of the Messiah—the counsel of the living God, particularly for those with "no ears to hear:"

> Wake up! . . . But if you do not wake up, I will come like a thief [to steal your wealth], and you will not know at what time I will come to you. Yet you have a few people in Sardis who have not soiled their clothes. They will walk with me, dressed in white, for they are worthy. He who overcomes will, like them, be dressed in white. . . . You say, "I am rich; I have acquired wealth and do not need a thing." But you do not realize that you are wretched, pitiful, poor, blind and naked. I counsel you to buy from me gold refined in the fire, so you can become rich; and wear white clothes, so you can cover your shameful nakedness; and have salve to put on your eyes, so you can see. Those whom I love I rebuke and discipline. So be earnest, and repent. Here I am! I stand at the door and knock. If anyone hears my voice and opens the door, I will come in and eat with him, and he with me. To him who overcomes, I will give the right to sit with me on my throne, just as I overcame and sat down with my Father on his throne. He who has an ear, let him hear what the Spirit says to the churches.

Now Revelation 3:7-13 addresses the Church from my birthplace in Philadelphia. Through an angel guiding this Messianic community, Yahshua, it is written, directed his servant John to write this "End Times" salvation message to whom it may concern. It directly speaks to my role as human coauthor of this book, along with, I suspect, this same angel:

> These are the words of him who is holy and true, who holds the key of David. What he opens no one can shut, and what he shuts no one can open. I know your deeds. See, I have placed before you an open door that no one can shut. I know that you have little strength, yet you have kept my word and have not denied my name. I will make those who are of the synagogue of Satan, who claim to be Jews though they are not, but are liars—I will make them come and fall down at your feet and acknowledge that I have loved you. Since you have kept my command to endure patiently, I will also keep you from the hour of trial that is going to come upon the whole world to test those who live on the earth. I am coming soon. Hold on to what you have, so that no one will take your crown. Him who overcomes I will make a pillar in the temple of my God. Never again will he leave it. I will write on him the name of my God and the name of the city of my God, the new Jerusalem, which is coming down out of heaven from my God; and I will also write on him my new name. He who has an ear, let him hear what the Spirit says to the churches.

The above counsel especially speaks to me. If you are unfamiliar with my work, let me to introduce myself, my biases, and why I am humbled to have coauthored this book.

My Hebrew name is Arya ben Schlomo ha Levi. That means "Lion of Yah [God's truer name], son of [Davidian King] Solomon, the Levi [priest]." I've never published my Hebrew name before. Most people simply know me as Dr. Len Horowitz. But sharing my roots seems appropriate for this special honor. It may help you understand why I've been so blessed to deliver this revelatory information at this interesting time.

I am best known for health science celebrity, having written dozens of scientific reports and more than 14 books, including the award-winning national best-seller, *Emerging Viruses: AIDS & Ebola—Nature, Accident or Intentional?* (1996) This politically charged text best explains the man-made origins of HIV/AIDS and Ebola. With stunning documentation, it scrutinized the genocidal origin of the world's worst plagues.

Rebuking false health doctrines and pharmaceutical deceptions since 1990, my wonderful wife, Jackie, and I have lived on a "roller coaster ride through the Twilight Zone." We gave up our relatively normal lives to pursue medical malfeasance and criminal injustices. I ended my sixteen-year career as a dentist, and fell from political grace as a nationally renowned health professional educator, to become a consumer health advocate and government whistle-blower. (See: www.originofAIDS.com and www.tetrahedron.org) I've been a repeat guest on every single one of those television networks I mentioned a moment ago. In a nut shell, I am widely known and respected for heralding many troubling truths about problems within medicine, in an effort to prevent disease and protect people, especially children, from those who abuse their power and economic might.

As a result of my notoriety and celebrity, many grassroots activists say a lot of kind things about me. You can read some of this on my official website—http://www.drlenhorowitz.com. One grassroots-activist turned investigative-journalist christened me the "King David of Natural Healing versus the Goliath of Slash, Burn and Poison Medicine" because of my actions in support of natural alternatives to deadly drugs. He had not known how inspired I was as a child when I heard the story of my tribal hero David versus the giant Goliath. Today, I earnestly petition Yah to open my heart to the fullest extent possible, with optimal Love and appreciation for His greatness, as my heroic ancestor David articulated so beautifully in Psalms.

Besides being a humanitarian and health professional, I do not consider myself very religious, just spiritually sensitive. Despite my Judeo-Christian leanings, I reject any religious exclusivity doctrines—Hebrew, Christian, or other. Such sectarian monopolization over salvation seems ridiculous to me. I believe going to church, mosque, or synagogue happens every morning when you open your eyes, take your first breath, and get your temple of Yah out of bed. Although I was reared Jewish, and love my Hebrew heritage, I married a Christian and thereafter opened my heart to Yahshua. I hold in my mind and heart tremendous respect for His sacrifice, ministry, and teachings, which showed the way to spiritual salvation for humanity. I view his teaching of The Way—*pure* Christianity—as a loving sect of Judaism focused on the Messiah's healing ministry and uplifting messages.

In recent years, as Overseer for The Royal Bloodline of David, I have dedicated much of efforts helping to build a virtual King Solomon's Temple for natural healing in the Hawaiian holy land we lovingly call "Sedona, Hawaii." Here, at "The Creator's Rainbow Spa," we are applying many of the ideas you will learn about in this book, for miraculous healing. The world is in need of exceptional models for sustainable living and natural healing. A major part of our mission is to create a venue for the science of creationism that you will learn about in pages ahead. For more information about this project, select apprenticeships, and work-study programs, visit www.steamventspa.com

To summarize my theology, I am multi-denominational, moderately spiritual, antagonistic to false doctrines of every kind, and feel greatly blessed to be guided to serve humanity in large ways.

In 1999, for example, I wrote the book *Healing Codes for the Biological Apocalypse* that revealed our omnipotent Creator's musical scale. This original series of six keys, the ancient Solfeggio, was secreted by my great ancestors, Levi priests on the other side of my family, around the time the twelve tribes of Israel fled the Holy Land.

As you will learn herein, this musical scale holds the "Key of David" to set our human family spiritually free. The two central tones in the scale are "Miracle 6" (528Hz) and the legally-appointed divinely-anointed "Family 9" (639Hz). You will learn more about this miraculous family frequency in *Walk on Water*, and the fact that David's key is vibrationally active in the "Star of David" (otherwise known as "Solomon's Seal"). King David always carried this special structure into battle while singing, in these tones apparently, or chanting Yah's praises. Featured herein is the knowledge that this six-pointed star is the sacred geometric form of molecular *water!* It is called "structured or 'clustered' water" in the scientific literature. I learned this, as did Japan's famous Dr. Masaru Emoto, from our water science mentor, Dr. Lee Lorenzen.

Years after working with Dr. Lorenzen, on a whim, I commissioned a genealogist to determine my family's crest-of-arms. I was stunned to see, front and center of the shield carried by my ancestors near the time the Templar fleet vanished from the port of La Rochelle, the six-sided hexagonal-shaped snowflake-like structure Dr. Emoto made famous in the documentary, "What the Bleep Do We Know™," and his awesome book, *The Message in Water: Love Thyself*.

Templar "pirates," who frequented Sardis, through their progeny, evolved economically, to become the world's wealthiest bankers and business leaders. I shared their history and New World Order trading agendas in my previous books, including *Death in the Air: Globalism, Terrorism and Toxic Warfare* (released June, 2001, that is, three months *before* the terrorist attacks of 9/11). *Death in the Air* examined leading "pirates" positions as powerful petrochemical–pharmaceutical profiteers. Obviously, these relatives of mine are the premiere source of our planet's pollution problems.

My last book, *DNA: Pirates of the Sacred Spiral (2004)* was written exclusively for intelligent lay persons and above, particularly health scientists and bioenergy enthusiasts. It merges spirituality with biology. This text too built upon scientific and scriptural revelations published in *Healing Codes for the Biological Apocalypse* (1999). *DNA: Pirates* vividly documents the threat to humanity, and myriad species, posed by the pirates genetic tinkering.

Now *Walk on Water* takes revelations in the aforementioned books to the next level featuring the most powerful dynamics and implications of the Creator's musical scale. As you will soon read, these Divine keys infuse water universally as the most extraordinary creative medium. You do not need to read my earlier books to gain great pleasure from these new revelations. However, you may feel compelled to peruse these earlier contributions once inspired by *Walk on Water*.

This book is necessarily technical in parts, although I have done my best to write here for the average lay reader. My challenge, and yours if you choose to read this book, is integrating recent advances in space/time physics, mathematics, and health science, with prophetic scripture. This exploration, like any pioneering effort, presents unique challenges to general audience communication for assimilation and appreciation of this information.

I celebrate and acknowledge angelic guidance in the authorship of this book. This work contains obvious Divine revelations. No man or woman alone could open these doors. No person, or physical force, can close them. These revelations derive from a source of inspiration and awareness beyond "normal" human reasoning. This publication is, therefore, both extraordinary and a sign of greater things and times to come. It evidences a spiritual revolution or renaissance Divine overtaking humanity with peaceful ingenuity, blessing exclusively the "righteous" and "faithful." All of this is very apparent in this labor of Love.

Signs and symptoms of this energetic aberration regularly occur for me and many people with whom I work. Since researching *Healing Codes for the Biological Apocalypse*, my computer searches, for instance, have often gone haywire to places I would never conceive of going.

Such was the case in preparing this Prologue when I researched Revelation 3. To my surprise, and delayed delight, my Bible software heralded Revelation 7 instead. It spoke to me like never before revealing for my first time the true meaning of the word "seal." Here is what this passage says will occur shortly before angels exact karmic justice among those "unsealed." Again, this is a warning to Templar progeny, recalcitrant "pirates," and others, who stubbornly violate nature's laws.

The forthcoming passage also heralds the Messiah's second reappearance. I have emphasized with *italics* certain words additionally revelatory as explained below. Rev. 7:1-4 speaks of the 144,000 who are expected to soon sing for planet-wide physical and spiritual salvation, and who are uniquely and divinely *sealed*. Now if you think Hurricane Katrina's wind and water warfare was devastating, "you ain't seen nothing yet." Here's a preview of second-coming attractions:

> I saw four angels standing at the four corners of the earth, holding back the four winds of the earth to prevent any wind from blowing on the land or on the sea or on any tree. Then I saw another angel coming up from the east, having the seal of the living God. He called out in a loud voice to the four angels who had been given power to harm the land and the sea: "Do not harm the land or the sea or the trees *until* we put a *seal* on the *foreheads* of the servants of our God." Then I heard the number of those who were sealed: 144,000 from all the tribes of Israel.

After naming all of the tribes, representing people worldwide of every religion, faith, and culture, gathered together for what I call the "Beginning Times Concert of the 144,000" (as per Revelation 14:1); during which time a "new song" will be sung to energetically uplift and restore Earth and those righteous to a more just state, or heavenly dimension, Rev. 7:9-17 describes these servants' purity of deeds and faiths this way:

> . . . [B]efore me was a great multitude that no one could count, from every nation, tribe, people and language, standing before the *throne* and in front of the Lamb. They were wearing white robes and were holding palm branches in their hands. And they cried out in a loud voice:
>
> "Salvation belongs to our God,
> who sits on the throne,
> and to the Lamb."
>
> . . . . These are they who have *come out of the great tribulation*; they have washed their robes and made them white in the *blood of the Lamb*. Therefore, "they are before the throne of God and serve him day and night in his *temple*; and he who sits on the throne will spread his tent over them. Never again will they hunger; never again will they thirst. The sun will not beat upon them, nor any scorching heat. For *the Lamb at the center of the throne will be their shepherd; he will lead them* to *springs of living water*. And God will wipe away every tear from their eyes."

What is the *seal* referred to here? What about these other emphasized words?

Webster's on-line dictionary defines "seal," the noun, as a fastener or device cut "to make an impression, used to secure a closing or to authenticate . . . . an indication of approved or superior status . . . a finishing coat [for] . . . perfect closure." The verb definitions include to "decide irrevocably."

By reading this book, you will learn that the *seal of the living God*, Yahshua, has to be referring to the powerful pure light and sound of Love moving through water. Not simply the waters of the world, including the water in your body—the holy temple—but water now found throughout the universe. Indeed, as per its definition, this *seal* is bringing Divine closure to the "great tribulation" in which the world is sadly steeped.

What else might we expect as a gift from the "Prince of Peace" on his return, but a technology for spiritual renewal through humble human vessels filled with Love. You will learn herein that these special frequencies of sound and light are the core creative and restorative vibrations of the universe. The evidence herein helps explain why these are exponentially increasing at this time, affecting life everywhere, but only strongly perceived by those humans who have been sealed, spiritually-sensitized, with "eyes to see" this Love light, and "ears to hear" this Divine calling. This melody in the true "key of Life," the "key of David," and the "key of Love." These are the spiritual sounds that made David's heart sing. This is also the seal of the living Yah who gave his life so that others may live perpetually on Earth as it is in heaven.

As you will soon learn, this seal is central to the spiritual renaissance. It is the spiritual coverage and energetic entrainment attracting you to the Source and service of creation. It is the most precious set of hydro-energetic, electromagnetic, and bioacoustic vibrations, frequencies, or resonances ever made. Their purpose is to attune and commune Creator to creation. The spiritual seal spoken of here is the powerful oscillating heart essence and core radiance of Yah. It is the bliss Apostle Paul experienced, and challenged everyone else to discover, by getting to know the true Spirit of the Creator. (1 Corinthians 2:6-16)

Why does the Bible say this seal is specifically on your forehead?

Because this is home to the pineal gland and site of the "third eye" that intuitively perceives things spiritually or energetically. Your pineal gland is a premier center for electromagnetic frequency reception, earthly orientation, and spiritual evolution. This is what birds, whales, dolphins, and myriad more species use to navigate and migrate thousands of miles so precisely without getting lost! Brain function and hormonal regulation critically depends on the bioenergetics and neuroendocrine dynamics of the pineal gland. David was smart for hitting Goliath right here. If you were to be spiritually guided and transformed into the likeness of Yah, "the seal of the living God" would have to be implanted here for you to receive Divine direction.

This also relates to the "Heavenly Throne." Herein you will learn that the throne of heaven is the matrix of everything—the universal source of creation at large. Our Creator sits upon this throne of creative potential and restorative energies, all the seals, the details of which will be presented herein. The purest set of matrix frequencies form the "Perfect Circle of Sound" that I have been privileged to herald since 1999 in advance of "The Beginning Times Concert."

The blood of the Lamb in Revelation refers to the sacrificial release of Yah's Holy Spirit to secure universal atonement; beginning from the ground up. Blood is composed principally of water—elements numbers 1 and 8, hydrogen and oxygen. It's red color comes from oxygenated hemoglobin. Blue blood lacks oxygen. This special element, and hydrogen too, vibrates or resonates with the primordial frequencies of Divinity. They, more than any other elements, cause the communion of matter and energy, spirit in matter, and God in man.

According to electromedicine experts, science focused exclusively on matter "covers only one billionth of all the phenomena in the Cosmos, and therefore draws unilateral and incorrect conclusions. . . . Resonance between oscillating particles is a primordial principle in the Cosmos." (*Journal of Bioelectromedicine.* Vol. 2, Number 2, June 2000, See: http://www.diamondhead.net/p2-2.htm) Therefore, it stands to reason that humans who are Divinely communed, preserved and protected in their primordial state, or *sealed*, must resonate in harmony with the Creator through, fundamentally, the blood, water, hydrogen, and oxygen.

Earlier, in *DNA Pirates of the Sacred Spiral*, I explained the roles and resonating capacities of these elements in electro-genetic expression.

"For the life of the flesh is in the blood," records Leviticus 17:11, "and I have given it to you on the alter, to make atonement for your souls. For it is the blood by reason of the life [force] that makes atonement."

Atonement means "at-one-ment," or becoming one with God. It also means "a-tone-ment" an *intended* tone, or musical key, played intentionally for divinity and community. In *DNA: Pirates of the Sacred Spiral*, I showed the genetic double helix to be a virtual antennae to God, to serve in this way as the receiver and transmitter of sound and light vibrations from this awesome source of intelligence.

If the Lamb is *at the center of the throne*, as Rev. 7 states, and His essence is Love—light frequency 518nm, and sound frequency 528Hz—then these frequencies must likewise emanate with His eminence from the center of the throne. You will review the first scientific proof of this fact, the specific frequencies at the center of the mathematical matrix of the universe, in this book.

Naturally, you would want this most loving core of Creation to be your guiding light for life. That is, you would want the living God to pull on your heart strings and *shepherd* you too to heaven on Earth; to the springs of living water. *Walk on Water* beautifully explains this longing for re-communing with nature and Source. Once you understand more clearly what water is, and the differences between energetically vital "living water" versus dead water which shortens life expectancy, you will better understand what this shepherding to the springs of the living water is really about.

To complete this prologue, I commanded my computer to recall Revelation 8. Once again, my software wildly *scrolled* to Revelation 5 instead which spoke to me about a sacred *scroll*. Rev, 5:1-5 touched my heart with this message:

> Then I saw in the right [outgoing and creative] hand of him who sat on the throne a scroll with writing on both sides and sealed with seven seals. And I saw a mighty angel proclaiming in a loud voice, "Who is worthy to break the seals and open the scroll?" But no one in heaven or on earth or under the earth could open the scroll or even look inside it. I wept and wept because no one was found who was worthy to open the scroll or look inside. Then one of the elders said to me, "Do not weep! See, the Lion of the tribe of Judah, the Root of David, has triumphed. He is able to open the scroll and its seven seals."

What is the scroll to be revealed only by the Lion of the tribe of Judah, with the Root and Key of David, guided by the angel blessing the Messianic community of Philadelphia—the "City of Brotherly Love," to opens doors that none can shut?

Herein, I advance a theory that the scroll is the outcome of Divine will, spin, and torque applied to the seat of creative power, that is, the throne, or mathematical matrix of the universe.

According to *Webster's* online-dictionary, "scroll" is defined as "a round shape formed by a series of concentric circles," like a spiral. You will learn herein that the entire universe is spiraling like a scroll relaying creative intelligence through simple mathematics. Math is the Creator's language. *Webster's* provides the computer definition of "scroll" as a "string [such as musical] and character recording oriented logogrammatic language." This pertains to the mathematics of language, or the alphanumerics of language, in which letters express the energy or spirit of certain numbers. This too is central to this book's main thesis: Our Creator is currently singing a mathematical musical language to crystallize creation and promote evolution. *Walk on Water* reveals the basis of this extraordinary language.

Thus, the Throne of heaven is the Creator's instrument played with loving heart strings and inspired breath. The scroll of the living God must result from this music and contain the Love and Law for creation inspired by the Creator.

In other words, the *Throne* is the instrument, the *scroll* is the sheet music, and you are part of the audience. From here you may be selected to play a role in the grand orchestra and have the Master Conductor and Supreme Composer direct your solo performance(s).

Furthermore, in mechanical engineering, *Webster's* says, a scroll means "a groove which winds itself into a spiral in the same plane." In *Walk on Water*, you will learn our groovy Creator winds himself into the spiraling double toroid structure of the universe from the same mathematical plane or dimension by expressing (or playing) certain keys formed from the special trinity of numbers 3, 6, and 9. Thusly, the "standing gravitational wave" of the universe is produced. Similarly, microscopically, your DNA mirrors this magnificent mathematical music fundamental to all laws of nature.

In essence, this book advances revelatory spiritual intelligence to return what was lost or suppressed, and restore what was missing or broken in hearts and lives. It is an accumulation and celebration of scientific facts that testify to the power, presence, and current processes by which our Creator is righting what went wrong with people and our planet.

The restoration of peace on Earth, decreed to be forthcoming in Revelation 21, involves "The New Jerusalem," or Yah-ru-sha-la-im in Hebrew and Chaldee (ancient Aramaic). Literally translated, this means "God's City of Peace." Experts say the name Jerusalem can be interpreted as the "foundation, vision, or possession of peace." Nearly everyone agrees that Jerusalem must fulfill its appointed destiny to become "the city of the Prince of peace," and "capital city of a world at peace," according to Bible scholar David Green. (See: http://www.bibletopics.com/biblestudy/47.htm) Before this occurs, however, the city must be "trampled" by spiritually-impoverished persons (Luke 21:24) as it is today. Soon, it will be restored to in the Messianic Age to become Yah's City of Peace. Here's a preview of your new life in the New World from Revelation 21:

I heard a loud voice from the throne saying, "Now the dwelling of God is with men, and he will live with them. They will be his people, and God himself will be with them and be their God. He will wipe every tear from their eyes. There will be no more death or mourning or crying or pain, for the old order of things has passed away." He who was seated on the throne said, "I am making everything new!

Then he said, "Write this down, for these words are trustworthy and true." He said to me: "It is done. I am the Alpha and the Omega, the Beginning and the End. To him who is thirsty I will give to drink without cost from the spring of the water of life. He who overcomes will inherit all this, and I will be his God and he will be my son. But the cowardly, the unbelieving, the vile, the murderers, the sexually immoral, those who practice magic arts, the idolaters and all liars—their place will be in the fiery lake of burning sulfur. This is the second death."

The "second death" refers to the massive population decimation predicted for the unprotected, the unsealed, reflecting back to the "first death" at the time of Noah in Genesis wherein to extinguish the dissonance and desecration of the Love vibration, Yah orchestrated the great flood. Water was used then to wash the people, plants, and things that were behaviorally unclear and spiritually unclean from the face of the Earth. Today, water is being used a bit differently by the Creator to accomplish the same result, as you are about to learn—a massive population annihilation (for the unsealed) and a grand spiritual awakening for a millennium of world peace for the remainder. Your fate in this mix is being now fixed.

Welcome to the world of *Walk on Water*.

Yours in the Spirit of Revelation,

Arya ben Schlomo ha Levi
a.k.a. Dr. Leonard Horowitz

XXVIII

Chapter One:
Introduction

The material you are about to read is the most important information I have ever shared pertaining to planetary salvation and spiritual evolution. I recognized the urgency of relaying this information to humanity when so many people are struggling to survive, questioning life's meaning, and wondering if God (I call our Creator "Yah") is still around to make good on promises to protect the faithful. Most prophets say we are in the "End Times." I agree, given the lame state of the world. Yet, this book brings great news for those chosen and/or choosing to receive it.

The focus of this book, the inspiration for this writing, is the underlying mechanics of spirituality and physical reality. The Bible predicts that in the "End Times," all of our Creator's greatest truths will be told. This book heralds revelations among our Creator's greatest, previously secreted, truths.

Due to the gravity of these revelations, I am compelled to share them. Yahshua said of his Hebrew family, "my people die from lack of applied knowledge," and the " truth shall set you free." The greatest truths hold the potential to set you the freest. I am, therefore, humbled to share these awesome truths at this urgent time; whereafter, I pray you will apply this knowledge for your physical salvation and spiritual evolution.

Due to recent developments in the fields of health science and mathematics, I felt it was essential to write a book that would share the underlying fundamental energetic basis and mechanics of life. I labored with love to write a book that would explain why scientific innovations that apply these truths hold the greatest potential to significantly impact healthcare throughout the world for centuries to come. Equally important, why science cannot be separated from spirituality particularly in healthcare. The information provided herein offers certain keys to understanding humanity's spiritual composition and creationistic evolution.

In 2001, I retired from professional broadcasting to seek the Kingdom of Heaven. Every morning as a news commentator and talk show host on World Wide Christian Radio (WWCR) I reviewed the *New York Times* and *Washington Post* to write my commentaries. For thirteen months, five days a week, this ritual focused my attention on bad news from "Babylon." Meanwhile, every one of my callers longed for peace and prosperity on earth. I realized that our focus on bad news prohibited us from researching the great news. So I retired in search of the keys to create heaven, versus hell, on earth. With this publication, I share the ripe sweet fruit of this labor of love.

The Need for an Alternative to "Modern Medicine"

Please allow me to set the stage for dispensing the great news by quickly exhausting the bad news in this brief section.

If you have lost as many friends and family members as I have to modern medicine and its toxic side effects, then you may be as delighted as I am to learn about successful alternatives.

During the past few decades, rapidly advancing and merging multidisciplinary fields of investigation, from biocosmology[1] and molecular biology, to mathematics and electrogenetics, have impacted health sciences and the natural health products industry in extraordinary ways.[2] The

"Nanotechnology Revolution," is changing everything. Add to this new theories and applications of evolutionary biophysics, that is, biology merged with creativity, and you have unprecedented research and development opportunities.[3]

These advances come at a time of great urgency. Biological innovation linked to spiritual recognition and human evolution is the only rational alternative to the ongoing devastation in medicine. I call this medical malfeasance, "iatrogenocide."[4] Without even considering the great grave toll attributable to vaccine injuries, medically-induced mortality and morbidity now ranks near the top of America's leading killers.

The catchy slogan, "Just say, 'No!' to drugs," does not apply to the Rockefeller-monopolized disease-care cartel.[2] Unethical, immoral, and criminal actions by Rockefeller cohorts demonized and generally alienated from society every alternative health discipline from chiropractic and homeopathy to acupuncture and herbology. This family, more than any other, sought and gained unparalleled power through the development of a disease care industry. They, more than any other, have created the great "End Times" plagues.

Without the general public's knowledge, the global drug cartel engages in the development of biological and chemical weapons of mass destruction for profit and population control.[5,6] Add to this substantial, if not complete, dominion over natural health resources with the rapidly advancing CODEX. CODEX alimentarius is the global policy affecting consumer access to vitamins, minerals, botanicals, and other natural medicines. And there is more malfeasance in the latest genetics/eugenics industry takeover of the "Human Genome Project" by these same "pirates." Thus, you have impending disaster.[7]

Figure 1. Greed and Deception in "Babylon"

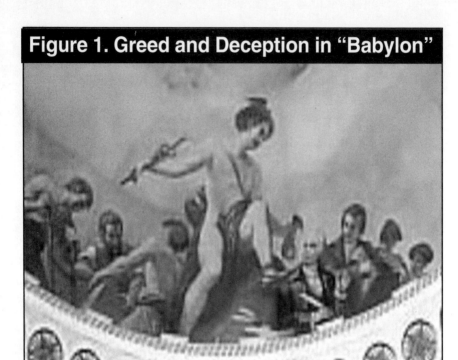

Dr. Horowitz shot this photograph in the Dome of the Rotunda of the Capitol Building in Washington the day before he testified on behalf of autistic children poisoned by mercury from vaccinations. It is a picture of the Greek god Mercury holding the medical insignia on his right, and a bag of gold on his left. Legislators look on with great interest for their political payoffs by the drug cartel.

Every life form now stands imperiled by this cartel's greed and malicious abuse of power. President Eisenhower, in his wisdom, warned us against this growing menace. Earth's people and the planet's entire ecosystem have now degenerated to the point of threatened extinction. Such is the multinational corporate threat posed by the Anglo-American oligarchy's military-medical-petrochemical-pharmaceutical cartel.[2,5,6,17]

Thus, humanity's need has never been greater for extended relief from this power-surge. We need to be set free from this generally-enslaving cultural addiction to drugs.[3] Our group mind has been set with mental illnesses, addictions, and passions as a poor substitute for Divine sustenance and existential bliss.

Innovations based on the information contained herein can help resolve these conflicts, and shall ultimately replace pharmaceuticals in state-of-the-art healthcare.

Walk on Water

Chapter Two:
Advancing "Biospiritual" Mathematics & Music

With the advent of nuclear-magnetic-resonance imaging (MRI) technology, healthcare engaged the field of biophysics. Bioresonating energy signals from machines caused recipients' cell nuclei to vibrate sending back signals to sensors that transformed this data to light energy electron flows on video screens.[8-10] This use of sound on body water to move nuclear matter is similar to the Creator's work eons ago in molding our universe.[9] This orchestra currently inspires your life.

Therapeutic uses for biosonics (i.e., biologically active sounds), including ultrasound, bioenergetics, and electromagnetism abound.[8-12] Anthropologically and medically, during the past few centuries, scientists worldwide gained great respect for physics and its psycho-spiritual specialty field called metaphysics. Monumental discoveries in physics and metaphysics are now causing paradigm shifts in the physical sciences.

For example, studies in structured water science, electrogenetics, and protein crystallography have provided awesome revelations about how you are built and operating. Your organic structuring is now recognized as being a manifestation or precipitation of energy into molecular sacred geometry.[13,14] Mathematical musical biophysics has proven to be fundamental to the observer and the observed in this deceptive physical world in which we live. As you will soon learn, everything is crystallized within water from math—the perfect language of the grand universal creative Spirit.[2]

People worldwide suffer a multitude of modern plagues for what reason? This new knowledge suggests illnesses initiate from degenerative resonances—too much or too little transmitted wave lengths and frequencies of energy (i.e., sound and light).

In the normal state, this bioresonant energy flows to and from every cell's DNA and along energy channels (i.e., meridians) that run throughout your body. This "life force" flows, ideally, in perfect balance with nature, or the universe-at-large.

This eternal force supersedes traditionally recognized cofactors for disease and death. Ailments for which drug-based methods of care have largely failed may be therapeutically amenable to bioenergetic advances. Modern medicine, which keeps patients under pharmaceutical duress, chemical dependence, and physiological and psychological addictions, has failed to provide optimal relief. New philosophies, products, and practices are emerging as low cost, no risk, effective alternatives.[3]

The "Human Potential Movement" of the sixties foreshadowed the "Natural Healing Movement" of today. Both correspond to the global "Consciousness Movement," and the more widely recognized "Spiritual Renaissance" and the Judeo-Christian Messianic paradigm. Impetus for these philosophical, theological, and metaphysical journeys towards enlightenment rests with the inadequacies of our troubled times.

The search for "meaning of life" is compelling. Today a popular focus is on spirituality and "spiritual healing." Medical sociologists teach during troubled times with life or death emergencies people increasingly turn to spiritual faiths to survive and even thrive. Where America now focuses its spirituality, even *Newsweek* tells us, is in heart felt prayer and practiced devotions. Yoga, meditations with deep breathing, chanting, praying, toning, speaking in tongues, and the martial arts all share the developing skill of communing with the Divine.[15]

The stage for revolutionary technical innovations in health-care has been set. "No pain, no gain!" Clamorous public demand exists for physical protections and spiritual ascension from cataclysmic events, Hurricane Katrina was one example.

Why then does mainstream medicine and the media principally feature biological warfare using vaccines, antibiotics, antivirals, antitumor agents, and radiation for disease control versus bioenergetic restoration through reharmonization with the foundational frequencies of nature, the lights and sounds of Heaven, yielding spontaneous, even miraculous, healing? Obviously, it's a matter of information and marketing. Profits come before people for politically-empowered drug makers.

For more than 5,000 years with simple acupuncture needles and herbs, oriental medicine efficiently rebalanced "human nature" by normalizing energy flow throughout the body. This Chinese tradition continues today with senior acupuncturists requiring payment *only* when their patients stay well. Acupuncture generally results in spontaneous remission of disease and healing without the substantial costs and risks of drugs. Why?

"There is nothing missing or broken in the Kingdom of Heaven," the Bible declares. Bringing Heaven to earth, like acupuncture, is a function of energy flow. It begins in your own enlightened (i.e., made light or spiritually etheric) "Temples." This message is eons old, advanced by earth's senior sages and Holy persons. Recently it has been embraced by multidisciplinary science. Let me explain.

The "Biospiritual" Mechanics of Life

The Holy Spirit, commonly recognized by all religions, uses the dynamics and mechanics of metaphysics to inspire life. Biophysics, the energy dynamics fundamental to biology and nature, is a subspecialty of metaphysics. Metaphysical theories and theologies go hand-and-hand with advancing reality theories and the physical sciences.

For instance, Russian physics scholar, Dr. Hartmut Müller, previously with the Institutes of the Russian Academy of Sciences and the Institute for Applied Mathematics of Leningrad University, proved that the human energy field, or "biofield," was entrained to a "standing gravitational force field" resonating from the periphery of the cosmos.[16] This field of study is mathematical and physical. It was christened "Biocosmology" by Chris King at the Department of Mathematics, at the University of Auckland, New Zealand.[1]

Müller et. al., showed that your body, like all biology, is mathematically generated piece by piece, or "fractally." Mathematically you crystallize or fall apart.[16,17] As an expert in space-time mathematics and physics Müller compared biological elements to cosmic elements: planets, galaxies and particles in space. Comparing double helix DNA to "the universe as a double helix on the logarithmic line," he concluded.,"[t]he genetic code itself is a product of the global standing gravitational wave = time wave."

By the way, waves flow according to certain laws in math.

Müller and colleagues detailed the existence of special "nodes" within which all physical elements congeal. From microscopic bacteria and cell organelle to macrocosmic celestial bodies and galaxies, all matter crystallizes in these special energy zones. He noted that this fractal (i.e., piecemeal) precipitation of matter is mathematically based on repeating sequences of the numbers 3, 6, and 9. This set of numbers is energetically, or spiritually, special, as you will soon see. The set opens the portal to the fourth dimension or spiritual domain. Müller wrote of a creationistic transition toward physical precipitation from spiritual ether—from the "unpacked medium" of disorganized or chaotic free energy to the "packed cluster medium" of physical objects in space/time.

This clustering or structuring of matter from free flowing particles in space, he wrote, was forced by a gravitational wave or grand "LIFEWAVE." Like water waves bouncing off the sides of a swimming pool, the grand LIFEWAVE is "refracted at the universe's light horizon." This slightly shifts the wave's direction and frequency, and each shift slightly modifies the position of the 3,6,9 dynamic number set. Müller figured out that the LIFEWAVE's bend was predictable. The bend is predicated upon this set of special numbers. Each place and time the grand LIFEWAVE hit the "light horizon" (virtual cosmic wall), its refraction shifted the 3,6, and 9 set (or energy portal's) position by a factor of "ln(6)." This number position of "ln(6)" relates to the biblical "in 6 days" for creation along the universe's logarithmic line as determined mathematically and experimentally by Müller and his colleagues as diagrammed in Figure 2.

As shown in this figure, the universal LIFEWAVE and the "standing wave" of double helix DNA are mathematically, logarithmically, and structurally correlated. Genetics, therefore, represents the physical crystallization of energized mathematical matter. This intelligence flows freely with mathematical precision. Energy flows with frequencies of sound (Hz) and wavelengths of light (nm), emanating force-fields affecting and connecting everything in the universe, you included.

Most fascinating to me is that the ln(6) LIFEWAVE phase, or complete sine wave cycle of universal creation, corresponds to the mathematics and harmonics of the original Solfeggio musical scale. These musical tones—sound frequencies—were encoded by my Levitical ancestors in the Bible's *Book of Numbers,* In the book *Healing Codes for the Biological Apocalypse,* these creative frequencies were revealed for the benefit of humanity.[17] As will be shown shortly, this mathematical music, sung from the depths of the cosmic ocean, creates the grand LIFEWAVE of Love that moves all matter. You included!

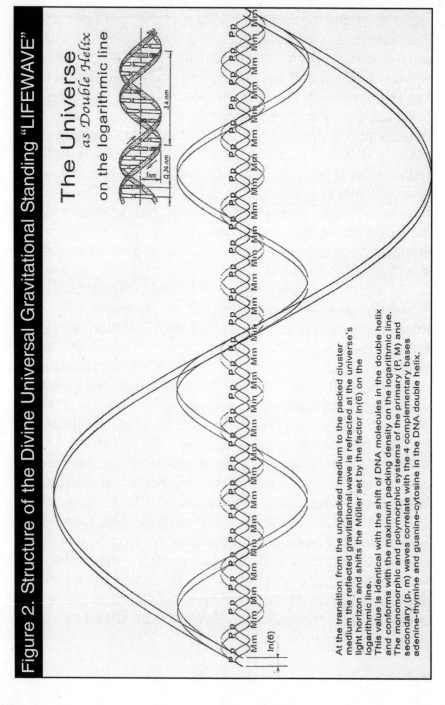

Figure 2. Structure of the Divine Universal Gravitational Standing "LIFEWAVE"

The Universe
as Double Helix
on the logarithmic line

34 nm

1nm

9.34 nm

ln(6)

At the transition from the unpacked medium to the packed cluster medium the reflected gravitational wave is refracted at the universe's light horizon and shifts the Müller set by the factor ln(6) on the logarithmic line.
This value is identical with the shift of DNA molecules in the double helix and conforms with the maximum packing density on the logarithmic line. The monomorphic and polymorphic systems of the primary (P, M) and secondary (p, m) waves correlate with the 4 complementary bases adenine-thymine and guanine-cytosine in the DNA double helix.

Chapter Three:
Divine Revelations
& "Healing Codes"

The book *Healing Codes for the Biological Apocalypse* advanced the ancient secreted original musical scale.[17] The book provided Bible passages related to the great spiritual battle described in Revelation 7:4 and Psalm 91 when the army of 144,000 servants of Yah take "refuge" in His "fortress" (Psalm 91:2-3). Only then, we are told, despite tens of thousands dying in their midst, all faithful will be delivered "from the snare of the fowler, and from the noisome pestilence." This same theme is repeated in Revelation 14:18 with the singing of a "new song" by this 144,000. The melody echoes throughout eternity and fulfills humanity's destiny to begin 1,000 years of world peace.

The word "peace" implies harmony versus dissonance. It naturally radiates from the mathematical musical matrix of being. It is the fruit of righteousness, that is, right-standing according to the mathematical laws of the universe.

The metaphorical "fortress" in Psalm 91 is this standing universal LIFEWAVE of Divine Love. It is strong enough to withstand any physical or spiritual force laid against it. The optimally righteous and faithful, those who hold "Love of Faith of Love" dearest, are instantaneously delivered from the trap sprung by the fowler to enslave humanity in the "End Times" and "Babylonian deception." The deceivers, Revelation 9:21 tells, practice "sorcery" and "cast magic spells." These literally reference pharmaceutical industrialists according to *Strong's Concordance*. They beat the hypnotic snare (i.e., television and the mainstream media) to poison humanity.

The foul filthy incarceration pertains to the "noisome pestilence" brought on by these drug pushers. This is the "noise," the pestilence" or "noisy dissonance," from which illness overtakes the sonically blessed and blissful "Temple." Shattering health, plagues are transmitted from the disturbing wave lengths and frequencies, including energetically-potent negative images and fearful thoughts, that oppose the Creator's universal LIFEWAVE and natural healing colors and sounds.

Deliverance of the chosen for the great "End Times" concert, prompting the long-awaited spiritual "paradigm shift," simply depends on the sound frequencies sung by a "critical mass" of faithful and trusting servants, according to the Bible's Revelation 14:1 and *Healing Codes for the Biological Apocalypse.*[17]

The 144,000 people represent a "FA-muli tuorum"—the *critical mass* of humble loving servants who sing in unison the notes of the ancient Solfeggio. As detailed in Table 1, this "Beginning Times Concert" will likely produce what was detailed in the book, *Healing Codes.* That is, the end of global population control, environmental pollution, and other "noiances" *Webster's Dictionary* refers to as "mathematical" problems. This concert instantaneously triggers the millennium of world peace.[17]

As shown in Table 2, these are also the tones with which to chant the hymn to Saint John the Baptist—believed to be the most spiritually uplifting hymn of all time. This sacred secreted music ends the global pollution of guilt and fear. A global transmission, now technologically possible, is all that is required.

These six "keys" unlock the door to optimal planetary freedom. They have precise definitions and frequencies shown in Tables 1 and 2, respectively. In summary, they include:

1) "UT"—the first tone that includes the "whole series of . . . musical notes" and the entire array of human emotions from grief to joy. That is, virtually the entire human condition all in one note! This note transmits a "magnetic field strength equal to 10^5 power gauss,"[17]

2) "RE"—the second key resonates a "relatively small periodic stimulus" in harmony with a much larger "natural vibration," to produce "a vibration of large amplitude . . . of enriched significance, profundity, and allusiveness," to "undo" the estrangement of mankind from "God-kind," and bring back the "earlier state of affairs." That is, return to the much desired "Garden of Eden," or manifest "Heaven on earth;"

3) "MI"—the miracle tone means "to produce an extraordinary occurrence that surpasses all known human powers or natural forces and is ascribed to a divine or supernatural cause esp. to God. . . ;"

4) "FA"—the fourth key heralds "the 144,000 servants equipped with this knowledge to be present to transact [this spiritual] business." In Christian terms, "FA" represents "the "bride" or "body of Christ." For Hebrews it is the Minyon required to raise the dead to spiritual life, or Yah's "chosen people." For Muslims it is the completely faithful servants of Allah. For the Hindus, it is Shiva's earthly army that cuts through the confusion;

5) "SO"—the fifth note shares this purpose. Solving the "mystery or puzzle," and working out "the answer or solution to [the] mathematical problem" underlying the "pollution" or spiritual dissonance; and the last key,

6) "LA"—means articulating, using the lips, the sounds required to "reverse direction" and move "toward extreme political conservatism." With conservation of matter and energy a supreme law in this logarithmically ordered universe, there is nothing more conservative than our Creator. This political movement and key unlocks the door "to an earlier system or order" that asserts world peace. This is the true meaning of Israel—where the "lion lies down with the lamb."

Table 1. *Webster's* Defined Solfeggio Tones Re: "Beginning Times Concert" for 144,000

UT–quent laxis

1. a syllable used for the first note in the diatonic scale in an early solminzation system and later replaced by do. 2. the syllable sung to this note in a medieval hymn to St. John the Baptist. <Gk. -Gamut- 1. the entire scale or range; *the Gamut of dramatic emotion from grief to joy.* 2. *the whole series of recognized musical notes* [1425-75]; late ME (Middle English)> <ML (Mediaeval Latin)– contraction, of *Gamma*, used to represent the first lowest tone of (G) in the Medieval Scale Ut, Re, Mi Fa, So, La, Si. <Gk -Gamma- 1. the *third* letter of the Greek alphabet. 2. the *third* in a series of items. 3. a star that is usually the third brightest of a constellation. 4. a unit of weight equal to one microgram. 5. **a unit of magnetic field strength equal to 10^5 power gauss**. (quent: needing), (laxis: loose; axis—an affiliation of two or more nations. Also Axis Powers.)

RE–sonare fibris (Res-o-nance)

1 a: the state of quality of being resonant. b (1) *a vibration of large amplitude in a mechanical or electrical system caused by a relatively small periodic stimulus of the same or nearly the same period as the natural vibration period of the system* 2. the prolongation of sound by reflection; reverberation. 3a. Amplification of a source of speech sounds, esp. of phonation, by sympathetic vibration of the air, esp. in the cavities of the mouth, nose and pharynx. b. a characteristic quality of a particular voice speech sound imparted by the distribution of amplitudes among the cavities of the head, chest, and throat. 4a. *a larger than normal vibration produced in response to a stimulus whose frequency is close to the natural frequency of the vibrating system, as an electrical circuit, in which a value much larger than average is maintained for a given frequency.* 5a. a quality of *enriched significance, profundity, or allusiveness; a poem has a resonance beyond its surface meaning.* 6. the chemical phenomenon in which the arrangements of the valance electrons of a molecule changes back and forth between two or more states. (in percussing for diagnostic purposes) a sound produced when air is present [1485-95]; <MF (Middle French), <L Resonantia, Echo = Reson (are) to resound + Antia-ance.(Re–a prefix, occurring orig. in loan words from Latin, use to form verbs denoting action in a backward direction , *Action in answer to or intended to undo a situation,* or that *performance of the new action brings back an earlier state of affairs.* (fibris: fibre string, vocal cord.)

MI–ra gestorum (Miracle)

1. *an extraordinary occurrence that surpasses all known human powers or natural forces and is ascribed to a divine or supernatural cause esp. to God.* 2. a superb or surpassing example of something; wonder, marvel [1125-75]; ME <L Miraculum=Mira(Ri) to wonder at. *fr* (French): sighting, aiming to hold against the light. (gestorum: gesture; movements to express thought, emotion; any action, *communication,* etc. intended for effect.)

FA–muli tuorum (Famulus,)

. . . plural Famuli, 1a. *servant/s, or attendant/s, esp. of a* s*cholar or a magician* [1830-40 <L (Latin), servant, of family. (Tourum - quorum - 1. *the number of members of a group required to be present to transact business or carry out an activity legally. usu. a majority.* 2. *a particularly chosen group.* [1425-75; <L quorum of whom; from a use of the word in commissions written in Latin specifying a quorum.)

SO-lve polluti (So-lve')

1. to find the answer or explanation for; clear-up; explain; to *solve a mystery* or puzzle, to work out the *answer or solution to (a mathematical problem.)* [1400-50; Late ME <L Solvere to loosen, release dissolve = so-var, after velarl, of se-set-luere to wash; (see Ablution.) Ablution n. 1. a cleansing with water or other liquid, esp. as a religious ritual. [1350-1400]. (Pollutii–pollute-luted, 1. to make foul or unclean,)

LA–bii reatum (Labi-al)

1. of pertaining to or resembling a Labium. 2. of pertaining to the lips, 3. (of a speech sound) *articulated using one or both lips.* 4. of or designating the surface of a tooth facing the lips. 5. the labial speech sound, esp. consonant, [1585-95]; ML lingual. (Reatum - reaction - 1. *a reverse movement or tendency; an action in a reverse direction or manner.* 2. *a movement toward extreme political conservatism*; 3. *a desire to return to an earlier system or order.* 3. action in response to some influence, event, etc.; 4. a psysiological response to an action or condition. b. a physiological change indicating sensitivity to a foreign matter.) 6. mech. the *instantaneous response of a system to an applied force*, manifested as the exertion of a force equal in magnitude, but opposite in direction, to the applied force [1635-45].

SI (Sancte Johannes)

1. a person of exceptional holiness, formally recognized by the Christian Church esp. by *Canonization.* 2. a person of great virtue or benevolence. 3. a founder or patron, as of a movement. 4. a member of any various Christian groups. 5. to acknowledge as a Saint. Canonize. [1150-1200]; ME Seinte. Canon: 1. an ecclesiastical rule or law enacted by a council or other competent authority and, in the Roman Catholic Church, approved by the Pope. 3. a body of rules, principles, or standards accepted as *axiomatic* and universally binding, esp. in a field of study of art.. 6. any officially recognized set of sacred books. 10. the part of the mass between Sanctus and the *communion.* 11. *consistent, note-for-note imitation of one melodic line by another, in which the second line starts after the first.* (axiomatic: 1. pertaining to or of *the nature of an axiom; self-evident.* 2. *a universally accepted principle or rule.* 3. *a proposition in logic or mathematics that is assumed without proof for the sake of studying consequences that follow from it.*

[Emphasis added in each definition denotes special relevance to the text, *Healing Codes for the Biological Apocalypse* **(1999), by Horowitz LG and Puleo J.]**

As seen in Table 2, by referencing these entries in *Webster's Dictionary*, "the original six notes of the Solfeggio compares closely to the meaning of the words and overall message in the hymn to John the Baptist."[17] This is how we win in the end, and those who are loving and meek shall inherit the earth.

Furthermore, Revelation 14:1-5 prophetically proclaims:

> Then I looked, and there before me was the Lamb, standing on Mount Zion, and with him 144,000 who had his name and his Father's name written on [or in] their foreheads. And I heard a sound from heaven like the roar of rushing waters and like a loud peal of thunder. The sound I heard was like that of harpists playing their harps. And they sang a new song before the throne and before the four living creatures and the elders. No one could learn the song except the 144,000 who had been redeemed from the earth. . . . No lie was found in their mouths; they are blameless.

These 144,000 sing to secure the Messianic Age for millions of others. As with the hymn to Saint John the Baptist this singing washes away guilt and fear from this polluted world."

Much like a water baptism, wherein a person is refreshed and blessed by the infusion of the Holy Spirit coming through water, this hymn, and others using the original Solfeggio tones, will instantly refresh and bless the entire planet. The intent here is to uplift human spiritual energy. The infusion of this same Holy Spirit power of Divine Love that knocked people off their feet upon the opening of King Solomon's Temple.

The Medieval Latin hymn records the 144,000 humble servants will need to sing in harmony with "the loose strings," that is, the logarithmic standing grand LIFEWAVE advanced by Müller et al., which will loose throughout the universe this awesome "roar of rushing waters." What a blessing![16]

Table 2. The Solfeggio Frequencies For the 144,000 "Beginning Times Concert"

1. Ut = 396 = 9   4. Fa = 639 = 9

2. Re = 417 = 3   5. Sol = 741 = 3

3. Mi = 528 = 6   6. La = 852 = 6

The Hymn to Saint John the Baptist

So that your servants
Can sing together
With the loose strings
The wonders of their deeds
Oh Saint John
Wash away the guilt
of their polluted lips.

Table shows the increasing frequencies encoded in the Bible in NUM-BERS, Chapter 7, verses 12–83. Initially encrypted by Levi priests who translated the original Torah into the Greek *Septuagint*, these six frequencies possess extraordinary spiritual power. Besides their link to the hymn to St. John the Baptist, and their likely association with creative and destructive events as detailed in the Bible, the third note—"Mi" for "Miracles" or "528"—is the exact frequency used by genetic engineers throughout the world to repair damaged DNA.[17]

These frequencies, as reported below, are unique to mathematics, physics, and Divine spirituality. It should be noted that these previously secret acoustic vibrations are the core resonant frequencies of the universe, and the primary ones associated with the matrix of creation and destruction.

These are the frequencies used by the Creator to form the cosmos in <u>six</u> (6) days, the "In(6)," as shown in Figure 3. The number 6 is universally important, as in "Carbon 6," the fundamental organic element and hexagonal ring (molecule) of life.

In the Book of Joshua, six (6) days of Levitical horn blasts followed by the Ark of the Covenant used as an energy amplifier shattered Jericho's great wall. During this time the people were instructed to remain completely silent so as not to alter the frequencies of these miraculous sounds. Then, on the 7th day the public shouted, and the walls "came tumbling down."

Additional evidence for the assertion of miraculous music comes from Rahab's story. In Joshua 2:21 she is instructed to apply a scarlet line to her window to spare her home, part of Jericho's great wall. In 6:17 she, her entire family, and her home was spared because of this action. In modern physics terms, the scarlet line acted as an acoustic/electromagnetic "heat sink" to absorb the miraculous, albeit destructive, energy blasts from the priests' horns.

This battle against the city of Jericho was not the last time these frequencies were used for war to destroy enemies. The third note of the musical scale—"Mi" for "Miracles," or "528"— is also the exact "Middle C" tuning fork frequency used by leading military weapons technicians today to tune their most sophisticated killing machines.[20]

Also, in the medical field, in the battle against genetic ailments, leading scientists use this frequency to repair "the blueprint of life," DNA.[17]

Theoretically, this genetic repair response is attributable to the fact that the 528Hz frequency is foundational to the grand universal LIFEWAVE, as well as to the DNA double helix. Thus, applying this sound to broken or mutated genetic material resonates the nucleic acids back to their original form and sequence, entraining them to the universal standing gravitational wave determined by Müller. You might say the broken or dissonant gene's frequency and wave length is modulated back to normal by the stronger "standing" resonance signals. In other words, the universe's fixed 528Hz frequency, central to Love, forces miraculous repair by harmonically vibrating the DNA strand back to normalcy. This is classic cymatic atunement.

The word "atonement" also has relevance. It implies communing fully with the core frequencies of Divinity, that is, resonating harmoniously with the universe's standing LIFEWAVE. It also means "at-one-ment," or the meaning of being in sync, at one, with the universe and its Creator. It can also mean "a-'tone'-meant," that is, the intentional production of a tone, and/or the hidden meaning of these tones as revealed in Table 1.

Like any technology, these frequencies may be used for better or worse, for good or evil, for creation or destruction. Reflecting again on Revelation 14:1, which is the first light in these "End Times" for humanity (i.e., at the interface between the darkness of Babylonian deception and the light of truth in the Messianic Age) comes this verse. It includes: "And I heard a sound from heaven like the roar of rushing waters and like a loud peal of thunder. The sound I heard was like that of harpists playing their harps."

The spiritually uplifting, enlightening, and entraining tone "from heaven" is "like the roar of rushing waters . . . ," a lion of a sound resonating from within superconducting water—the creative medium through which sound precipitates matter and energy.

"Darkness and light" Genesis records, heaven and earth, and even the universal firmament or ether emerges hydroacoustically. All this began with the sound of the Creator's words, core acoustic frequencies, on water.

In this aqueous creative and recreative medium, the sound of global restoration and physical salvation is heard, "like a loud peal of thunder," made by cracking electrical currents connecting earth and sky, heaven and earth, like lightening.

This "End Times"/"Beginning Times" sound "was like that of harpists playing their harps." This is prophetically linked to weather and water changes in the Book of Revelation, as well as the energetics of physical salvation and spiritual evolution.

Might this have anything to do with the superstorms of the new millennium, earth and weather changes? Research strongly indicates the U.S. Government's HAARP project, heating the atmosphere in an era of global warming, is a weather modification instrument played for politics and economics, curiously fulfilling this Bible prophesy.[6]

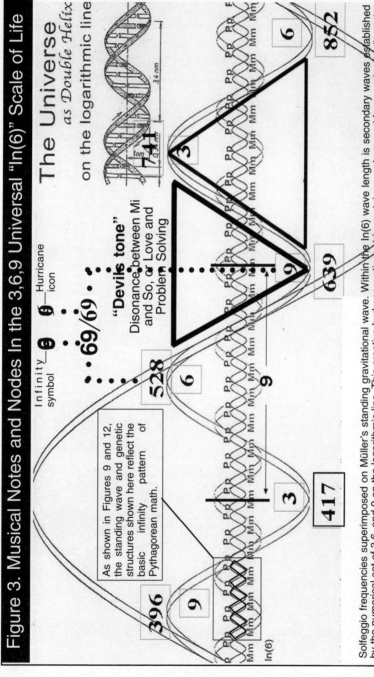

Figure 3. Musical Notes and Nodes In the 3,6,9 Universal "ln(6)" Scale of Life

The Universe
as Double Helix
on the logarithmic line

Infinity symbol
Hurricane icon

69/69

"Devils tone"
Disonance between Mi and So, or Love and Problem Solving

As shown in Figures 9 and 12, the standing wave and genetic structures shown here reflect the basic infinity pattern of Pythagorean math.

Solfeggio frequencies superimposed on Müller's standing gravitational wave. Within the ln(6) wave length is secondary waves established by the numerical set of 3,6, and 9 on the logarithmic line. This creative hydroacoustic matrix contains numbers and frequencies to direct the flow of crystallized matter; its form and function. Wave phases vary tone expressions affect everything. The dissonant frequencies 528Hz and 741Hz is known in music as the "Devil's tone." Between 528Hz and 639Hz, the center of the "LIFEWAVE," Love and Family vibrations predominate. Theoretically, the universe is shifting into this more harmonious phase of the wave, which might explain the Spiritual Renaissance.

Walk on Water

Chapter Four:
Davidian Music in the Key of Life

The Bible's *Book of Revelation* records the transition from Babylonian dissonance, deception, disease, and discord to the Messianic Age—a thousand years of world peace. This grand performance—an energy cycle forced by the mathematics of the Creator's rhythm—alters the mood and temperament of the audience throughout this period. Music can do this as you well know. Imagine the power of Divine music played by the universal orchestra on your health and well being. Planetary consciousness and spiritual evolution is, likewise, affected.

Notice in Figure 3, that the 528Hz frequency tone resonates near the center of the grand LIFEWAVE adjacent the 639Hz harmonic. These two adjacent frequencies resolve in Pythagorean mystery school mathematics to 6 and 9, respectively. For instance with 639, 6+3+9=18; and 1+8=9. These are symbols for the alpha and the omega, yin and yang— "69." The combined symbols also represents the Picean balance. Merge these two numbers to form the infinity symbol or the figure 8. Interesting also, using Times Roman font, this symbol represents the "Eye of the Hurricane" (**ᕼ**) or the knowledge that everything in the universe is spinning like a hurricane. This is, likewise, associated with galactic clusters and the double toroid structure of the universe according to recent discoveries to be discussed later.[2]

Please understand that these flat diagrams of wave dynamics in Figures 2 and 3 crudely represent hyper-dimensional physics. The actual spiraling water and double helix contains periodic sound frequencies which harmonize with, or conversely interfere with, tones of different nodes emanating in all dimensions. Visualizing these vibrational energies within and around each DNA strand, and the universe at large, facilitates understanding of the (cymatic) forces crystallizing physical reality. (Cymatics will be explained later in Chapter Seven. Proof of the mathematical patterning of genetic structuring will also be presented later.)

This material precipitation features the sacred geometry of hexagonal organic chemistry and more. Imagine here the forces of various frequency interactions creating three dimensional tetrahedron-shaped water molecules. These flow into the shape of Solomon's Seal (the "Star of David") and the Merkaba, (a nine-pointed star reflecting the ancient sun symbol) as water molecules cluster for optimal electrogenetic function. All of these patterns and more occur within the double helix heavily influenced by third adjacent triangulated tones.

All of these combined frequencies form major, minor, augmented or diminished triads resonate from within to without– "as above, so below." These chords of creation move material matter, physical forms or crystallizations, along paths of least resistance throughout the energized aqueous ether of space/time.

Figure 4 shows the technological innovation called the "3E™" that I developed with these understandings. The 3E™ is the abbreviation for "Evolutionary Energy Enhancer." (See: www.healthyworlddistributing.com.) This simple technology incorporates the core frequencies for creationism, that is, "The Perfect Circle of Sound," first advanced in *Healing Codes for the Biological Apocalypse*. (See: http://www.3epower.us.)

This mathematically-confluent sequence of notes was used by internationally renowned toning expert, Jonathan Goldman, to produce a tuning fork set from which the amazing CD entitled "Holy Harmony" was recorded. (See: www.healthyworlddistributing.com.) Accompanied by these forks struck in an ascending manner, Goldman's vocalists chanted the Hebrew letters of the Messiah's name to these "Healing Codes." Goldman intuited years ago "the use of these forks in this particular manner creates a sacred spiral that seems to encode itself as a matrix upon the cellular structure, and particularly on the DNA. I believe this is the matrix of

Figure 4. "3E™" Evolutionary Energy Enhancer: Keys of Life and Essential Frequencies of Divinity

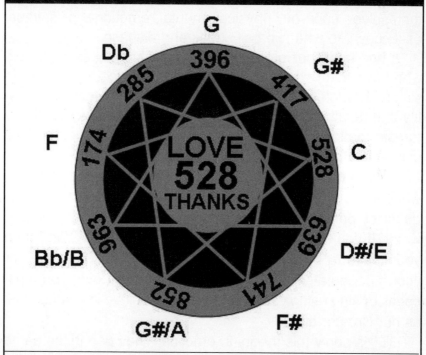

These are the core frequencies for universal creation. Evidence for this assertion is detailed below with the works of Rodin and Haramein. (See Figure 10 and discussions in Chapters Six and Seven.) These frequencies are also believed to open a portal to the fourth dimension, or spiritual realm. Exclusive usage of 3E™ technology with positive loving intent must be considered "experimental."

the 'higher' human—helping create an evolutionary step in our genetic encoding," he wrote.[18]

Goldman further reported that his experience using the vibrational fields generated by these tones, when used in ascending or descending order, "seems to have the ability to nullify any frequencies that are counter productive to our highest good. These frequencies create a blanket of Divine sounds that may counter the effects of harmful energy including bacteria and viruses." Without making medical claims, Goldman reported these frequencies likely nullify and dissipate disharmonious energies that may be trying to establish themselves upon our physical, mental, emotional or spiritual essences into what we call stress and disease.

It has been our great pleasure to bear witness to people who have told us astounding stories of healing that occurred simply through listening to 'Holy Harmony.' We can also testify that health care practitioners have recorded extraordinary transformational and healing experiences with clients while using the Holy Harmony CD and/or tuning forks.[18]

Now, before returning to the 3E™, recall the world began when the Creator's "word" acted on water. That is, sound frequencies based on physics and mathematics were applied to water. If you, and I, were created in the "image of Yah," then your lips must be your co-creative instruments. Therefore, for you to cooperatively recreate this world with Love, you must speak or sing using your lips to project this love into water, just as our Creator did.

3E™s apply this theory in practice. They use these same mathematics, harmonics, and geometrics to impart these frequencies into water to energize it and the world beyond. In this way, water can be "programmed" with powerful prayerful messages of love, thanks, peace, health, and prosperity. Simply personalize it with your own creative affirmative heartfelt prayer.

Each of the frequencies of the ancient Solfeggio on the circumference of the 3E™s radiates one of the three primary colors: blue, red and yellow. 396, 417 and 852 are blue; 528, 963, and 174 are red; 639, 741, and 285 are yellow. These color energies spin off from the grand LIFEWAVE and vibrate your genetics. Your DNA spins and amplifies these frequency signals with torque blending them to form the other key colors: green, orange and purple. As our Creator used these colorful tones to manifest miracles, so too can you use them now to cooperatively create a better and healthier world.

Many people are already experiencing enhanced spirituality and miraculous manifestations in their daily lives by using the Holy Harmony CD, the tuning forks, and the 3E™.

My main objective in developing the 3E™ was to enhance and widely distribute "Love power" to benefit all life forms on this ailing planet. .

3E™ applications should only be intended to contribute to the Spiritual Renaissance and help facilitate healing and the Messianic Age for people from all walks of life to enjoy.

Warning: *Attempts to use this technology with bad intent will backfire!*

Energizing Water for Healing

Since 3E™s were developed to inspire water, you can spiritually bless your body—a vessel nearly 80 percent water—with these loving messages, positive intent, special thanks, and sound frequencies. 3E™s may be used on, or off your body, alone, or in combination, with other bioenergizing technologies,[3] toning, sacred music and/or prayer, to promote structur-

29

ing (or "clustering") of water,[13] enhance genetic signaling,[2] and prompt spiritual atunement for personal and global healing.

With prayer and loving intent, 3E™ stickers can be placed on acupressure points to stimulate desired outcomes. Apply the stickers, or reusable "cling-ons," to water glasses and other water containers. Float four-inch 3E™s on water in swimming pools and ponds to resonate thousands of gallons of water at once. Put them on computer screens, windows, and windshields to vibrate the aqueous atmosphere. Each time you apply these stickers you transmit a signal of "LOVE" and "THANKS," to miraculously repair DNA and bless your mostly liquid body and our entire atmosphere.

Using 3E™ technology in these simple ways derives from scientific and Biblical revelations supporting the theory that these special numbers carry an energy signature. In fact, everything carries an energy signature since everything is created by sound and light energies. These precise numbers, however, exclusively reflect the awesome power and glory of our Creator, and His law directing all creation through the grand unification, the universal LIFEWAVE. The Creator's creations are perfect by nature as they comply with these mathematical laws. Entrainment to these Divine frequencies occurs best in water, a superconductor.

These frequencies of music open the mathematical "portal" to the Divine realm, "universal consciousness," and the greatest force in the universe known to science, that is, the standing gravitational LIFEWAVE.

This may be understood in terms of Judeo-Christian theology as our Creator's spiritual energy, commonly referred to as the Holy Spirit. This is omnipresent and increasingly helpful in this era of earthly renewal.

Ancient myths and all religions declare water fundamental for life and all creation. Scientists from many fields now agree that pure water, composed of molecules with sacred geometric forms (i.e., tetrahedrons and their 3D derivatives including Soloman's seal and the Merkaba), relays frequencies of sound and light, much like crystals do, to inspire nature. This is primarily how genetic inheritance is expressed and reality is precipitated in a quantum field, or matrix of energy, the firmamental ether referred to in the Bible's *Book of Genesis.*

Many of the world's leading energy experts—geniuses like Albert Einstein and Nicola Tesla—likened such creative processes and energy to Divine spirituality. They worked to free humanity from enslaving conditions, particularly ignorance of simple, math-based, laws of physics and nature.

Could pure water, and simple technologies, like the 3E™, affect water purity and resonance? Could these mathematical symbols and words emit energies to affect personal and global purification and healing? Modern science, ancient scripture, and eons of experience cumulatively say, "Yes!"

Indeed, there is great creative and curative power in subtle vibrations affecting water's "hydroelectricity," molecular structure, and signaling capacity. The genetic strands shown in Figure 5 were published in the journal *Science.* These photographs show DNA's hydroelectrically-affected energy (i.e., spiritual or electrical potential) studied by geneticists from the University of California at Berkeley.[24] The top photos show DNA bathing in energetically-blessed structured (clustered) water. This kind of water is commonly found in healing springs and in mothers' breast milk. These hydrated double helixes hold far greater energy potentials than the same strands of DNA shown below them. Dehydration caused the difference.

This dehydration experiment proves that a slight reduction of energized water bathing genetic matrices causes DNA to destructure, fold, and energetically fail. That is, these creation-

Figure 5. Electromagnetic Functions of DNA & Clustered Water On Cellular Metabolic and Structural

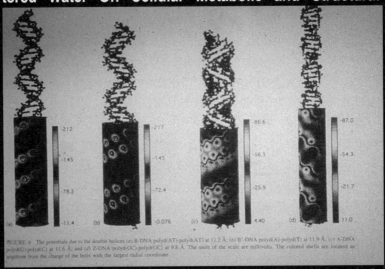

FIGURE 4 The potentials due to the double helices (a) B-DNA polyd(AT)·polyd(AT) at 11.2 Å; (b) B'-DNA polyd(A)·polyd(T) at 11.9 Å; (c) A-DNA polyd(G)·polyd(C) at 11.6 Å; and (d) Z-DNA polyd(GC)·polyd(GC) at 9.8 Å. The units of the scale are millivolts. The colored shells are located in angstroms from the charge of the helix with the largest radial coordinate.

Electrical potentials in millivolts of adequately hydrated DNA are shown in the figures above. Saykally et. al, showed small clustered water rings, mostly six-sided, facilitate electromagnetic transmissions to and from the double helix.

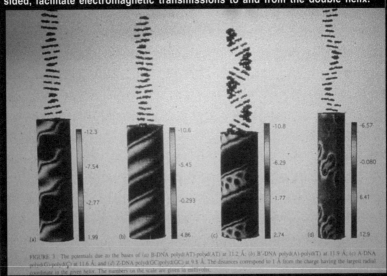

FIGURE 3 The potentials due to the bases of (a) B-DNA polyd(AT)·polyd(AT) at 11.2 Å; (b) B'-DNA polyd(A)·polyd(T) at 11.9 Å; (c) A-DNA polyd(G)·polyd(C) at 11.6 Å; and (d) Z-DNA polyd(GC)·polyd(GC) at 9.8 Å. The distances correspond to 1 Å from the charge having the largest radial coordinate in the given helix. The numbers on the scale are given in millivolts.

The figures above show the results of water cluster dehydration on DNA, and resulting drops in millivolt potentials degrading cell signaling (i.e., frequency upregulation for structural integrity and metabolic functioning). Besides greater electrical potentials, the upper figure clearly shows more pronounced frequency transmissions reflected in the well formed patterns in the associated radial photographs. Source: K Liu, JD Cruzan and RJ Saykally. Water Clusters. *Science* (16 Feb) 1996;271:929-931.

istic antennae regress by dehydration accompanied by electrical degeneration and molecular entropy preceding physical degradation.

Besides playing a key role in electrogenetic signaling, water's subtle energy transmissions underlie the success of myriad healthcare practices from homeopathy and acupuncture to advanced biotechnologies such as magnetic resonance imaging (MRI) and Rife frequency generators.

Planetary protection and healing, most scientists now agree, derives from waters involved in purification and natural cleanup. Surely, water is our planet's most precious, creative, and healing resource.

In *The Message from Water*, water's astonishing ability to transform its structure in response to human emotions and heartfelt intentions was advanced. Shown in Figure 6 are photomicrographs contributed by Dr. Masaru Emoto. These structures appear to change in response to prayers, and words such as "LOVE" and "THANKS." This simply means that words—mathematical frequencies—affect the nature, structuring, energy carrying, and creative signaling capacities of water. Spiritually blessed water is Divinely structured (or organically organized) into mainly hexagonal rings as shown in this figure.

Inspired by these revelations, Dr. Emoto dedicated his life to preserving precious water purity. He works to prevent extinction of the human race and various other life forms still surprisingly surviving on this chemically beleaguered planet. He recommends writing the words "LOVE" and "THANKS" on water containers to relay these hopeful messages to the water to benefit its resonance and all of us. Thus, 3E™s contain these words along with the 528Hz core Love frequency of the universe.

Figure 6. The Difference Between Structured Water Containing "LOVE" Energy Versus Polluted Water

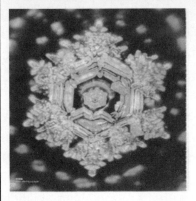

These water photomicrographs were all taken at 20,000 magnification by Dr. Masuru Emoto. Left side photos show the six-sided, hexagonal-shaped, snowflake-like, water structures associated with the healing waters of the world. They differ significantly from polluted waters shown on the right below. Dr. Emoto's co-investigator, Dr. Lee Lorenzen, concluded "clustered" waters maintain an energy signature suitable for optimal electrogenetic (DNA) function, longevity, and healing.

Alternatively, waters polluted by chemical toxins such as chlorine and fluoride, pesticides, or heavy metals, lose their sacred geometric water rings, and their vibrant energy signatures. Following municipal water treatment, drinking waters appear like raw sewage, as shown here, compared to the Divinely-inspired healing waters of the world. Dr. Emoto learned that water structuring also depends on human consciousness and positive intent.

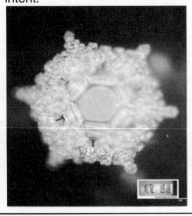

Water that is prayed over with loving, or otherwise positive, intent enhances its structuring. The photo on the left demonstrates this amazing aqueous ability. Alternatively, geometrically structured water cursed verbally or from dissonant/chaotic modern "music," deforms and grossly degerates into muddy structures like that seen in the photo above. For more information about this field, read Dr. Masuru Emoto's book, *The Message from Water*, Tokyo: Hadu Publishing, 2001.

Implications for Survival & Spiritual Evolution

The implications of this information are myriad and urgent for our planet's ecosystem—our common survival. This intelligence compels reconsideration of the manner in which our sacred creative liquid—water—is being abused, poisoned, and energetically retarded by adding chlorine, fluoride, and other toxic substances in the name of "public health" and industrial enterprise.

We need to stop polluting our waters! Especially since there are more intelligent and cost-saving ways to naturally protect us from waterborne diseases. These include oxygenation and ultraviolet light technologies.

The middle photomicrograph shown in Figure 6 represents the class of chemically and/or psychoenergetically poisoned waters. Its crystallized cluster appears unstructured and in disarray. Compare this to the other photos. **Which water would you prefer to drink?**

For optimizing your health and wellness through proper water consumption, fasting, improved nutrition, and much more, I highly recommend that you read *Healing Celebrations: Miraculous Recoveries Through Ancient Scripture, Natural Medicine, and Modern Science.* (See: www.healthyworld-distributing.com. A great summary of this book may be found on the Internet at: http://www.healingcelebrations.com.)

You need to purify and reenergize poisoned and electrically-depleted water before drinking it. Why? Because you are actually an organic spirit-filled expression of waters' highest qualities. You are, as Dr. Emoto asserts, "a messenger relaying love and thanks to others." This message echoes throughout the cosmos for all those with ears and hearts open to receive.

The urgency of our threatened existence compels us to use our knowledge of water science to develop new technologies for our common survival. The 3E™ was invented with these common concerns, and purposes, in heart and mind.

Simple, yet powerful, 3E™ technology is offered with the heartfelt loving intent to contribute to the rapidly accelerating Spiritual Renaissance and planetary purification process. Theoretically, by inspiring our waters, and our bodies mostly made of water, with the core frequencies of universal creation, and the sacred geometry reflecting this "Perfect Circle of Sound," we will call forth from within the realm of Divine creative intelligence the evolutionary energy needed to secure love, peace, health, and prosperity for ourselves and our entire planet for generations to come.

Chapter Five:
Phi, the Golden Mean,
and Music Uplifting Life

Advanced herein is a complete musical mathematical model of the universe. Goldman explained how special the ancient Solfeggio scale is, and how it may be used for healing. He noted the 417 and 528Hz frequencies of the second and third notes resonate together to "create an interval very close to the Phi ratio found in the Fibonacci Series." This ratio, related to the Golden Mean, is mathematically linked to the sacred spiral of sound—your DNA.[2,18]

In *DNA: Pirates of the Sacred Spiral*, I wrote of the "Mathematical/Musical Oneness" of "Creative Consciousness."[2] "Your DNA," I noted, "receives energy from this domain and relays this universal essence through bioacoustic/electromagnetic signals." In this way, "Yah's energy," or what many people call "universal consciousness," is relayed to humanity and shared by all life forms. This "I am" communing presence of light and love holds the resonant frequencies of the Creator's colors. Personally expressed by your choice and co-creative power, this Divine rainbow warms hearts, uplifts spirits, and bathes everyone and everything in sacred sounds of harmonious Oneness.

DNA, your sacred spiral, incorporates these sounds, colors, and the geometric form known as the Golden Section. This mathematically and geometrically special Golden Section is harmonically attuned to the Fibonacci series of numbers, 34 and 21, due to the fact that each full cycle of DNA's double helix spiral measures 34 angstroms long by 21 angstroms wide. Their ratio, 1.6190476, is very close to phi (ϕ) — 1.6180339.

This musical mathematics determines the sacred geometry of DNA. It is a perfect five-sided pentagon for each helical spiral of the molecule. Double this to construct the twin helix, with each full helical spiral rotating 36 degrees, and you end up with a decagon formed from the two pentagons as shown in Figure 7. (It is not likely coincidental that the highest level possible in the hierarchy of the global elite's secret society, Freemasonry, is also 36; wherein 3+6=9 or completion in Pythagorean mystery school math.)

DNA expresses this mathematical musical perfection. The molecular structure, as shown in Figures 5 and 7, results from the "Perfect Circle of Sound." Genetic structure also corresponds to the ascending or descending tones according to Phi ratio analysis and Rodin's mathematical infinity pattern as shown in Figures 9 and 10.

This uncommon knowledge about DNA's structure, based on perfect musical mathematics, helps to explain your physical structure as well. (It also explains why you love music!) For example, your pentagonal body shape, with two arms, two legs, and a head, results from resonance frequencies of energy manifested through pentagonal-shaped genetic antennae. All is in Divine proportion to the Golden Mean (0.618). Again, DNA's cross section is based on Phi (ϕ). The ratio of the diagonal of a pentagon to its side is ϕ-to-one.[2]

Thus, as shown in Figure 7, no matter which way you look at it, even in its smallest segment, DNA, and life, is constructed using Phi, the golden section, and the "Perfect Circle of Sound."[19]

Figure 8 depicts a typical chord chart composed of triads for major, minor, and seventh cords. Allow your eyes to engage the flow of musical notes on the staff. This produces the visual impression of the music moving as a double wave much like that of DNA. The main difference is DNA spirals in three dimensions in hydrated cells while music flows through humidified air. In both instances, transmission is affected by varying amounts and qualities of water.

With this intelligence, you can now see that the creator's musical signature is fundamental to every living organism containing DNA. In fact, the Golden Section, or Phi, is found throughout nature. This reflects the relationship between the Creator and all of creation. How so?

There is only one way a line may be divided so that its parts are proportional to, or reflected by, the image of the whole. Only by "tri-viding" the whole is the "mathematical relationship of component parts to the whole preserved," wrote The Phi Nest group.[19] This is much like our theological understanding of the Trinity. We are said to be created in the Creator's image, filled with the Holy Spirit, and kin to the Father and "Prince of Peace."

The ancient symbol for Phi itself is informative. It consists of a single circle and a single line through its center. The circle alone, mathematically, symbolizes zero. Theologically, this represents nothing or nothingness.

Nothingness extending eternally includes everything. Think about it. If nothing expanded everywhere at the same time, then it would include all matter and energy. Then there would be nothing else, and nothing would include, if not be, everything!

The same is true for everything. Everything expanded eternally leaves no room for anything else and, therefore, yields nothing.

So, everything and nothing are contextually the same as the yin and yang, the good versus evil, the male versus female, the light versus darkness polarity of the universe. One cannot exist without the other.

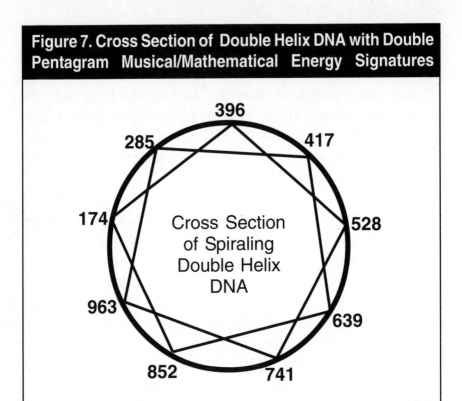

Figure 7. Cross Section of Double Helix DNA with Double Pentagram Musical/Mathematical Energy Signatures

Cross Section of Spiraling Double Helix DNA

396
285 417
174 528
963
639
852 741

Figure 7 results from connecting keys in the "Perfect Circle of Sound" that correspond to the ascending or descending tones in Rodin's mathematical infinity pattern as shown in Figure 10, and according to Phi ratio analysis.

In ancient theology, a simple line between two points represents unity or communion with the Divine Source. The nothing (everything) symbol, zero, split by the line of unity, yields the Greek letter Phi— ϕ —denoting the Golden Number or Golden Mean. It reflects your Divine connection to the cosmos, and is the mathematical and structural essence of DNA. These combined symbols help explain the Creator's electro-

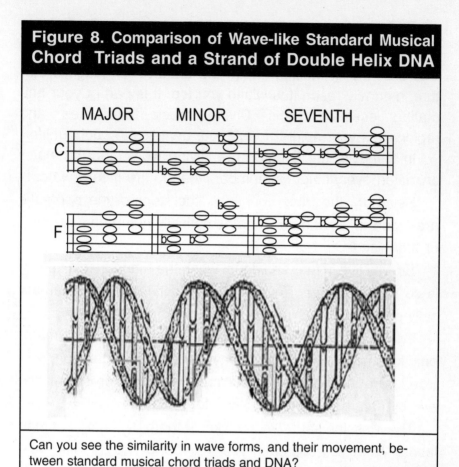

Figure 8. Comparison of Wave-like Standard Musical Chord Triads and a Strand of Double Helix DNA

Can you see the similarity in wave forms, and their movement, between standard musical chord triads and DNA?

magnetic and bioacoustic relationship to humanity, and all of creation, expressed through the mathematical constant 1.618, and DNA.

Adding zero to one in this way is, not surprisingly, the beginning of the Fibonacci series.

Music, principally written using these two ancient theological and mathematical symbols (i.e., ovals and lines), also reflects and facilitates Divine communion.

Divine Wisdom and Musical Unity

The essence of musical math, the creative language of nature, naturally resonates within you too. It is part of your animating essence. This Divine music expresses and replenishes your spirit through your genetics throughout life.

In Genesis, the Creator, the Divine word, and the water animated everything. Remember, you too are mostly water.

Relatedly, the Bible counsels, "the steps of the *righteous* are ordered." That means mathematically numbered, aligned, or organized.

So why live in fear and doubt when the Kingdom of Heaven is so near and dear, musically manifesting, and mathematically precise?

These same sound frequencies from the musical/mathematical matrix, the perfect heavenly source of creation, provides pure inspiration for your creative self expression. You are, by nature, a powerful cocreator.

The Messiah said, "Ye shall know them by the fruit of their labor." What you cocreate, your harvest of "fruit" in life, best defines you. Yahshua also said, "You will be judged by every word you speak." Your words either reflect Love in your heart, or "the evil that dwells therein."

This far reaching discussion involving music, mathematics, Love, and creative self-expression relates also to "original sin." Here's how:

The English language is alphanumerically related to sacred Hebrew but backwards.[17] "LIVE" spelled backwards is "EVIL." The Garden of *Eden* spelled backwards is the garden of the *nede* (or needy). While you choose to *live* in your head versus your heart, in fear and doubt rather than trust and Love, you alienate yourself from Divine grace and *Eden*'s garden wherein your sustenance is freely and continuously provided. You become "Nede" and need to labor ceaselessly for your sustenance while feeling alone rather than inspired and supplied (as the *righteous* are) by Divine communion through the mathematical matrix and Holy Spiritual connection.

Herein lies the original sin—the duality option is yours. You have the choice to know in your heart you are mathematically-Divinely connected and ordered. Hereby your harvest, the "fruit" of your labor, is easily obtained. Alternatively, you can choose to remain ideologically disconnected, seemingly alone, mentally stressed, and physically needy. The choice is yours.

These truths have been metaphorically expressed throughout the ages in poetry, prose, religious scripture, and even Hollywood movies. In "Yellow Submarine," for instance, peaceful loving civilization is enslaved simply by putting a stop to their music. By freeing silenced "Sergeant Pepper's Lonely Hearts Club Band," and rebroadcasting their simple melodies—"all you need is Love, . . . Love, . . . Love," humanity transforms from lifeless black-and-white to blissfully reanimated living color.[2]

Walk on Water

Chapter Six:
The Creator's "Signature"
on Everything Imparts Love

A recent breakthrough in mathematics by Marko Rodin perfectly compliments the "Healing Codes" revelations, the musicology advanced by Goldman et al., and the space/time physics of Müller and others.[16-19]

The logarithmic view of the universe musically unfolding within a standing gravitational wave, or grand LIFEWAVE, can be most readily appreciated by studying Rodin's math. Rodin's math proves the core creative frequencies are those of the ancient Solfeggio. This math science additionally reinforces the certainty of our Bible code discoveries, and the theory underlying 3E™ technology.

Rodin independently discovered the original musical frequencies, without knowing it, in his master mathematical matrix viewed in Figure 10.

These specific hidden number patterns, Rodin realized, touch every part of reality from black holes to blood cells. All matter, in other words, displays this math at a most fundamental, yet complex, level.[2]

The Creator's mathematical language manifests everything in the universe as independently confirmed by these works.[16,17,19,25]

The full nine (9) note sequence, 174 through 963, includes: 1 7 4, 2 8 5, __ 9 __, 4 __ __, __ 2 __, 6 __ __, 7 __ 1, 8 __ __, 9 6 3. (Fill in the blanks to reveal the "Perfect Circle of Sound," a continuously rotating number sequence. For help, refer to the 3E™ diagram in Figure 4.)

Using the base ten number system, as is done in Pythagorean math, with nine as the zenith and multiple digit integers added to derive their single digit between one and nine, Rodin studied several interesting patterns. Doubling these numbers, one through nine beginning with one, yields the pattern 1,2,4,8,7,5 infinitely (i.e., 1+1=2; 2+2=4; 4+4=8; 8+8=16 and 1+6=7; 16+16=32 and 3+2=5; 32+32=64 and 6+4=10 and 1+0=1; 1+1=2, etc.). When dividing by two, this pattern is also produced, but in the reverse direction. This offers a bit of insight into the math underlying nature and balanced polarity wherein mirroring multiples are evident.

Rodin used these patterns to develop the topology of a toroid named after him. According to Rodin's patterns and toroid, the numbers three, nine, and six—not present in the infinity pattern—actually create the fourth dimension as mapped in the accompanying Figures 9 and 10. Rodin likens his mathematical map to "God's fingerprint" since it appears in every facet of the universe.

Physicist Nassim Haramein further developed this concept modifying Einstein's field equations with considerations given to torque, spin, and polarity. He derived the double toroidal concept of the mathematically perfect universe, as depicted in Figure 10, to help explain his "Grand Unification Theory."[25]

The implications of these discoveries, like the universe, are limitless. Vastly beneficial creative potential rests in the application of this knowledge to solve humanity's greatest problems. One likelihood, most exciting to both Rodin and Haramein, is the generation of free energy to liberate us from petrochemical reliance, economic slavery, and environmental toxicity.

The universe is constantly spinning and torquing with energy. Tapping it was proven possible by Tesla. His technology was secreted by the energy industrialists.[6]

Figure 9. The Infinity Pattern and Separate 3,6,9 Triangle

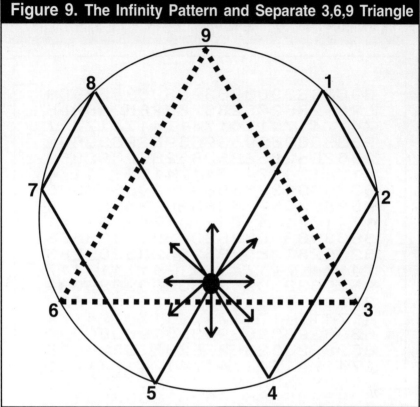

Rodin studied several interesting mathematical patterns. Doubling numbers beginning with one (1) yields the pattern 1,2,4,8,7,5 to infinity. When dividing by two, this pattern is also produced, but in the reverse direction.

Ths infinity pattern depicted here provides a unidimensional template for multi-dimensional DNA. It also projects the mathematical matrix or template of the universe as shown in Figure 10. This simple discovery offers the essential mathematical formula underlying nature, balance, and unity as detailed by Rodin and Haramein.[25]

The numbers 3, 6 and 9 provide a completely distinct triangular pattern which, according to Rodin and others, presents a portal to the fourth dimension, or spiritual realm.

The infinity pattern 1,2,4,8,7,5 diagram is structurally identical to the standing gravitational wave (the grand LIFEWAVE) of the universe and, at the microscopic level, your DNA as shown in Figure 12.

Figure 10. Rodin's Mathematical Toroid Infinity Pattern Independently Determined to Include the Ancient Solfeggio Tones

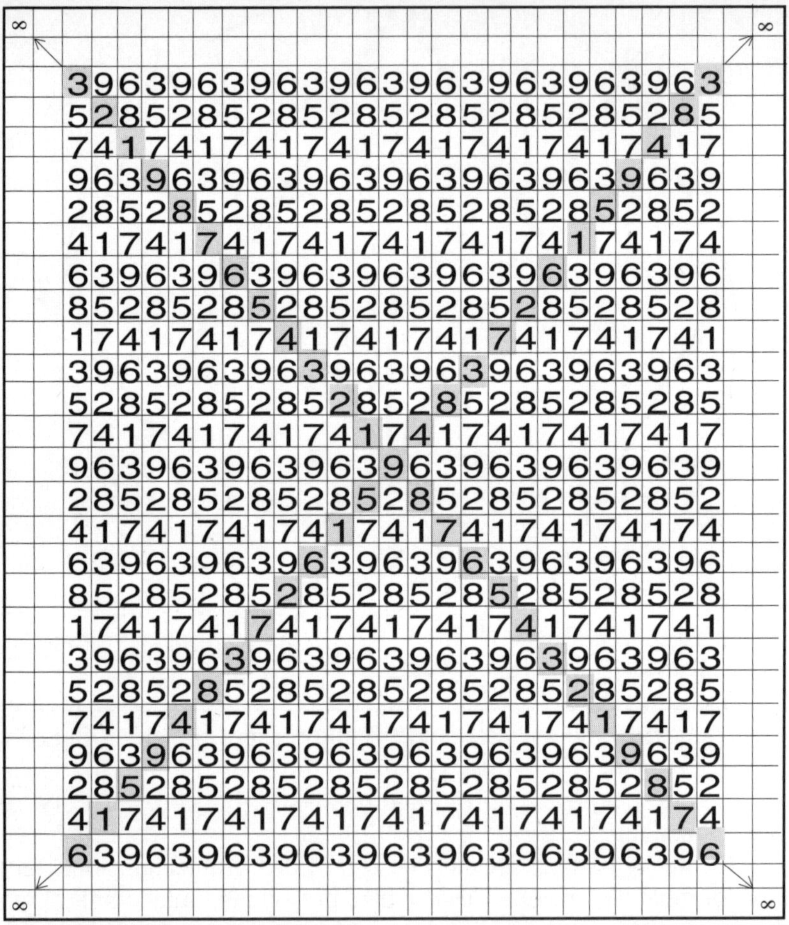

After corroborating Rodin's and Haramein's monumental works, many great minds from the fields of physics, biology, chemistry, and even computer science, have been able to resolve enigmas in their fields by understanding the Creator's unique, all encompassing, mathematical system.

Figure 11. Haramein's "Grand Unification Theory" Graphic of Double Toroidal Universe[25]

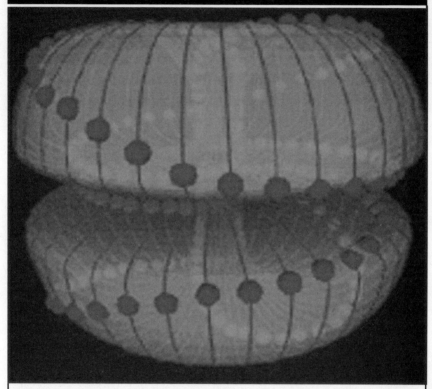

Haramein's thesis is discussed at http://www.theresonanceproject.org and http://www.theresonanceproject.org/interviews/nassimbayarea.mp3 [25]

Cocreating Your Reality

These advances have helped us comprehend the physics, and universal energy dynamics, of creative consciousness. If you have ever wondered how certain life experiences including synchronistic miraculous manifestations and prayed-for outcomes occur for you in space/time, these works provide a clue. With your DNA entrained to the mathematical matrix of the grand LIFEWAVE, your neurology powered by this energy, and your thoughts and imaginings likewise enabled, energetic transmissions from your heart/mind, as well as your lips, travel throughout the cosmos considering the Grand Unification Theory. Herein, these energized messages acquire additional torque, spin, and polarities. Like magnets they attract their opposite charge, or repel realities similarly charged.

Table 3. Stable Intervals of Set "3,6,9" on the Logarithmic Line Expressed in Cell Organelle

Cell Organelle Measuring Unit:		m	n(0)	n(1)	n(2)	n(3)	n(4)	n(5)	n(6)	n(7) Remainder
Protrusions	Inf:	0.000000007	18	-e-1						-4.00
	Sub:	0.000000009	18	-6						-6.35
Oxisomes	Inf:	0.000000007	18	-e-1						-4.00
	Sub:	0.000000009	18	-6						-6.35
Membrane (thickness)	Inf:	5.1E-09	18	-e-1						-2.73
	Sub:	0.00000001	18	-9						-8.42
Preribosomes	Inf:	0.000000006	18	-e-1						-3.26
	Sub:	0.000000015	18	33						32.85
Ribosomes	Inf:	0.000000021	18	6						8.48
	Sub:	0.00000003	18	e+1						3.50
Cilia (thickness)	Inf:	0.00000024	21	-18						-18.79
	Sub:	0.00000026	21	-42						-42.06
Lysosomes	Inf:	0.00000045	21	6						5.82
	Sub:	0.0000005	21	e+1						3.52
Peroxisomes	Inf:	0.00000021	21	-e-1						-2.80
	Sub:	0.0000009	21	6						5.82
Nucleolus	Inf:	0.000001	21	-6						-5.34
	Sub:	0.000002	21	15						14.79
Golgi vacuoles	Inf:	0.00000011	21							20.08
	Sub:	0.0000021	24							23.02
Mitochondria	Inf:	0.0000003	21							21.08
	Sub:	0.000003	24							23.38
Cilia (length)	Inf:	0.0000051	24	-30						-30.76
	Sub:	0.00001	24	e+1						4.65
Cell nuclei	Inf:	0.000003	24	-e-1						-4.39
	Sub:	0.00001	24	e-1						4.65
Cells	Inf:	0.00003	24							23.38
	Sub:	0.0003	27							27.99

In Müller's thesis, the logarithmic line of the standing gravititational wave is vital for all creation in that throughout the universe matter only crystalizes in locations of nodal resonance, or energy concentrations. These involve what Nikola Tesla heralded as the powers of the 3s, 6s, and 9s. Shown above are the mass measurements of cell organelle that follow this pattern.[16]

Table 4. Stable Intervals of Set "3,6,9" on the Logarithmic Line Expressed in Celestial Bodies

Celestial Body	Measuring Unit	m	n(0)	n(1)	n(2)	n(3)	n(4)	n(5)	n(6)	n(7)	Remainder
			Orbits of Planets And Some Moons								
Phobos	Inf:	58932900	54	-269							-268,17
	Sub:	58934750	54	-270							-269,03
Deimos	Inf:	147403500	54	e+1	-e-1	-48	62				61,26
	Sub:	147403600	54	e+1	-e-1	-48	162				162,35
Andrastea	Inf:	802991050	57	-6	-e-1	6	9	-e-1	-18		-18,40
	Sub:	802991100	57	-6	-e-1	6	9	-e-1	-9		-8,13
Amalthea	Inf:	1139139200	57	-57	e+1	-e-1	e+1	9			8,40
	Sub:	1139139300	57	-57	e+1	-e-1	e+1	6			6,53
Thebe	Inf:	1392982000	57	18	-14						-13,97
	Sub:	1400000000	57	18	-e-1						-3,57
Moon	Inf:	2413418500	57	e+1	18	-15					-15,93
	Sub:	2413435100	57	e+1	18	-17					-16,43
Io	Inf:	2648990900	57	e+1	-9	-72	-42				-42,60
	Sub:	2648991000	57	e+1	-9	-72	-8				-7,32
Mercury	Inf:	3,59E+11	63	-9	-14						-13,58
	Sub:	3,61E+11	63	-9	-8						-7,22
Venus	Inf:	6,75E+11	63	9	-e-1	e+1	93				93,13
	Sub:	6,77E+11	63	9	-e-1	e+1	-e-1				-3,27
Earth	Inf:	9,43E+11	63	e+1	9	-e-1	e+1				3,33
	Sub:	9,44E+11	63	e+1	9	-e-1	12				11,51
Mars	Inf:	1,31E+12	63	e+1	-e-1	e+1	-e-1	e+1			2,88
	Sub:	1,3E+12	63	e+1	-e-1	e+1	-e-1	8			7,72
Jupiter	Inf:	5E+12	66	-e-1	-6						-6,96
	Sub:	4,8E+12	66	-e-1	-18						-17,92
Saturn	Inf:	8,9E+12	66	-32							-31,99
	Sub:	9,1E+12	66	-44							-43,32

As with cell organelle listed in Table 3, Müller's data also shows cosmic creations, in this case celestial bodies including all planets in our solar system, abide by the mathematical laws regulating the logarithmic standing gravititational wave and physical reality. Matter only crystallizes in locations of nodal resonance, or energy concentrations, involving 3, 6 and 9 metaphysical mathematics.[16]

In this way, loving versus coldhearted intent cuts to the core of the universe effecting your creative/attractive capacity. Thus, experiences can be either attracted or repelled depending on what you transmit, positive or negative!

This helps explain "karmic laws" of Divine judgment and universal balance. It helps explain how you are judged by every word that comes from your mouth, as the Prince of Peace decreed in Matthew 12:36: "I tell you this, on the Day of Judg-

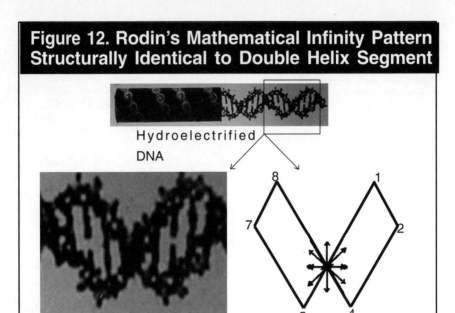

Figure 12. Rodin's Mathematical Infinity Pattern Structurally Identical to Double Helix Segment

Hydroelectrified DNA

As seen in Figure 9, a diagram of the infinity pattern 1,2,4,8,7,5 is structurally identical to each segment of DNA spiralling in the double helix. Adjacent segments flip sides and possibly even polarities to accelerate energy flow and electrogenetic signal reception and transmission. Again, this same structure appears in Figure 3 in the framework of the standing gravitational wave (the grand LIFEWAVE.)

Thus, "as above, so below." What is true for the macrocosm, is true for the microcosm. The entire universe is perfectly pattered mathematically, the same way throughout, empowered, enabled, and restored exclusively by Divine mathematical design.[16]

ment people will have to give account for every careless word they have spoken; for by your own words you will be acquitted, and by your own words you will be condemned." The same seems reasonable for your thoughts and imaginings, especially during these days of spiritual awakening, Divine atunement, and cocreative manifestation.

These works by Müller, Rodin, and Haramein also help explain the phrase, "As above, so below." This math is constant throughout the macrocosm and microcosm. As shown in

Tables 3 and 4, Müller found all celestial bodies and cell organelle, in fact all of physical creation, share predetermined physical characteristics based on this fundamental mathematics and metaphysics. Detailed technical treatments of this important subject are available from Müller[16] and Haramein.[25]

Given this evidence, it is likely that each cell with a genetic blueprint of the universe operates with equal intelligence. Individually and as groups, cells can be relied upon to respond intelligently to mathematical input. That is, electromagnetic and bioacoustic input (i.e., creative stimuli) including your thoughts and visualized prayers (i.e., visualizations).

This mind-body-spirit connection, potentiating even cellular psychosomatic reactions, also best explains human healing by placebo as well as its opposite called "nocebo"—the disease-triggering reaction initiated by ignorant physicians..

Nocebo related ailments may be commonly caused by frightfully negative disease "labels"—poor prognostications and urgent or deadly professional proclamations. Fearful patients are thus prone to health professional manipulations subject to their disease labels (e.g., "terminally ill"). Such labels actually become illness cofactors, or risk factors, in increasing morbidity and mortality.

Alternatively, recognizing the structural biodynamics—the bioenergetics of life—and the fact that all diseases might be more conscientiously considered energy imbalances, professionals might commonly inform patients of this overriding influence and address their educational and lifestyle change needs prior to prescribing slash, burn and/or poison forms of "modern medicine."

Obviously, these considerations and revelations hold profound significance for transforming healthcare.

The Greatest Risk of Genetic Engineering

From Haramein's "Grand Unification Theory" and this sacred secreted understanding of the mathematical basis of modern physics and biocosmology comes recognition of the grossest risk from genetic engineering. Müller et al., determined DNA is in perfect nodal resonance with the Universal LIFEWAVE.[16] Therefore, with the universe mathematically unified, and energetically harmonized with DNA, tinkering with earth's "genetic pool" is sending distress signals out to the edge of the universe.

The dissonance of genetic engineering, its pan-generational derangements, and resulting devolution, with threatened species extinctions, also runs contrary to natural selection based on frequency-based or vibrational creationism.

The harmonious alignment of universal energies forming the double helix is being violated worldwide by genetic engineers. Thus, man-made mutations oppose natural conservation of matter and energy. This universal law is being broken with genetic engineering as DNA is being mutated and human electrogenetics devolves.

This increased risk of species extinction is echoing throughout the universe. Genetic tinkering can now be seen to have cosmic ramifications. Spiritually sensitive beings throughout the cosmos would surely feel this challenge to universal integrity.[2,16]

If you were an enlightened loving extraterrestrial, even Yah, thriving on universal spiritual energy, and years ago you began to perceive that something on earth, or someone here, was altering or damaging your natural sustenance, creating dissonance or change in the dynamics of the Divine plan, you might be seriously alarmed by this. You might consider conducting a search and rescue mission, and probably figure out a way to help generally clueless earthlings. You might realize earth's people were unlikely to survive due to their ignorance.

This is not what geneticists technically call "apoptosis," genetically programmed cell death. This is profitable biomedical *omnicide*—genocide for all species.

You would likely engage these deadly and unnatural forces in ways earthlings misunderstand, including experimental abductions. These have been widely reported and contested.

I believe that if we have an extraterrestrial or spiritual presence on this planet, it most likely sources from this genetic insult to intelligence and universal integrity.

Equally insane, Figure 15 shows photographs of scientific efforts to construct extraterrestrial super-mutant infectious agents—viruses in space! These have been brought back to earth for study. This foreboding abuse of technology now threatens us with alien viral outbreaks potentially causing multiple species extinctions. Humanity is especially threatened with decimation and demise. As if we do not have enough health risks!

As televised, drink your beer, pop your pills, stay hypnotized, and kiss life good-bye as you know it.

Can you see more clearly now how and why, whether you like it or not, you are engaged in "spiritual warfare," and why only a mass awakening, or spiritual renaissance, offers salvation? This Divine revolution is upon us, and is urgently timed.

Love Manifestations of the Divine LIFEWAVE

Table 4 lists the masses and dimensions of human cell organelle mathematically analyzed by Müller. "Without exception, measured dimensions of cell organelles are found within the stable intervals +18, +21, +24 and +27." Again, these resolve into the Pythagorean integers 9, 3, 6 and 9 on the logarithmic line. All cell organelle, like all stars and planets throughout the cosmos, Müller showed, prefer these specific subintervals within the grand LIFEWAVE. Müller labeled these (e+1) and (e-1). According to Müller, this arrangement allows for maximum flexibility in size. It is particularly remarkable that cell nuclei, containing the greatest amount of genetic material, precisely occupy the complete stable interval of +24 harmonically fixed by the ln(6).[16]

As noted in Figure 3, the logarithmically fixed ln(6) is centrally associated with the 528Hz (Mi6) frequency of sound. This frequency, according to clustered water pioneer, Lee Lorenzen, and others,[21] represents the miraculous repair frequency for damaged DNA. As mentioned, this tone would hold this genetic repair capacity only because its frequency is central to that of the universal standing gravitational wave and the natural vibration of harmoniously resonating double helix DNA. The repair outcome is assured by the law of entrainment whereby the stronger magnitude standing universal wave, or grand LIFEWAVE, modulates the spontaneous genetic repair capacity through the 528Hz core genetic frequency.

In other words, DNA—the "sacred spiral"—is resonating continuously back into its natural shape by the Creator's logarithmic force field. Sound vibrations from the core of the universe align the double helix for optimal energy reception, transmission, and health.

Now consider the fact that 528Hz, the "Mi6" tone, is the third note of the ancient original Solfeggio musical scale. It is also the frequency equivalent to 518nM of light in the electromagnetic color spectrum.[31] This precise center of the rainbow is also the core of the color green, the chakra of your heart, wherein love is most strongly resonant and felt.

Figure 13. Proof of Water Throughout Space

NASA photograph of evaporating ice particles in the tail and surrounding the nucleus of Comet Hyakutake. This proves water abounds throughout space and the entire universe in various phases. Investigators conclude this water is the matter from which cosmic bodies crystallize.
Source: *Astrobiology Magazine*, 2001.

With this knowledge, you might better appreciate the abundant greenery of planet earth as a "Love offering," quite literally. Nature's greenery directly reflects the central loving essence of our Creator's music and grace, also expressed through your heart. All of this is attuned to the grand LIFEW-AVE of mathematical/musical design.

This scientific revelation evidences the center of your heart is energetically attuned to the center of the universe! Its fundamental drive, or message—"Love"—is both personal and universal.

This knowledge also supports the conclusion reached by water scientist, Masaru Emoto, who independently concluded the "Message From Water is Love Thyself."[13]

In 2001, astronomers determined for the first time that water in the cold regions of space manifests in frozen *and* gaseous forms. (See: Figure 12.) "This is especially interesting," *Astrobiology Magazine* reported on the NASA project, "because these regions are the future birthplaces of low-mass stars like the Sun, and solar systems like our own." Space researchers concluded this determination, "underscores the fact that prebiotic conditions seem to be widespread" throughout the universe.[29]

So science now proves the Bible's *Book of Genesis* is technically accurate. Everything was created, and still exists, from sound and creative goodness directed through water.

In summary, the central message reverberating throughout hydro-energized space/time, the premiere creative flow within and throughout the aqueous universe, and the core dynamic of your heart's center, is "Love."[13]

As the Spiritual Renaissance hastens from the increased expression of this 528Hz central portion of the grand LIFEWAVE, this change, central to your DNA, must cause a human metamorphosis towards expressing more Love.

Annually, geneticists learn new ways DNA is being expressed. New blood factors, endorphins, and hormones are discovered yearly, all regulated electrogenetically, that is, biospiritually. As the grand LIFEWAVE increasingly expresses its central Love and family frequencies, 528Hz and 639Hz, in these "End Times," you and I must physically respond or die.

When children reach puberty they grow dramatically transforming into mature adults capable of bringing new life to earth. A LIFEWAVE activated, genetically modulated, blood-factor regulated metamorphosis is simultaneously taking place. It accompanies a great global spiritual awakening. From this, we human "caterpillars" are being transformed into divine "butterflies."

Chapter Seven:
Creation Through Sound Vibration

German investigator Peter Pettersson is an expert in "cymatics" — the study of sound on matter. He effectively summarized the creative connection between sound vibrations and physical reality by reviewing the work of the field's top researchers. His work laid the foundation for scientifically comprehending creationism.[2]

Pettersson began with Ernst Chladni, the first observer of the shapes and forms produced as a result of sound vibrations striking the surface of matter. Chladni was, not surprisingly, a musician and physicist. Born in 1756, he laid the foundations for the discipline within physics called acoustics—the science of sound.

In 1787, Chladni published *Discoveries Concerning the Theory of Music*. In this and other pioneering works he explained ways to make sound waves generate visible structures. "With the help of a violin bow which he drew perpendicularly across the edge of flat plates covered with sand," Pettersson wrote, Chladni "produced those patterns and shapes which today go by the term Chladni figures." This was significant because it demonstrated that sound actually affected physical matter. It held the power to create geometric forms in substances.

Later, in 1815, Nathaniel Bowditch, an American mathematician, further advanced Chladni's work. He studied "the patterns created by the intersection of two sine curves whose axises are perpendicular to each other, sometimes called "Bowditch curves," but more often "Lissajous figures," . . . after the French mathematician Jules-Antoine Lissajous. Both

Bowditch and Lissajous concluded that the condition for these designs to arise was that the frequencies, or oscillations per second, of both curves stood in simple whole-number ratios to each other, such as 1:1, 1:2, 1:3, and so on.

In fact, one can produce Lissajous figures even if the frequencies are not in perfect, but close, whole-number ratios to each other, Bowditch reported. "If the difference is insignificant, the phenomenon that arises is that the designs keep changing their appearance."

This knowledge, applied to electromedicine, provides tremendous potential for healing virtually every illness.[17,28] Much like 528Hz resonates a DNA strand back to normalcy, cymatics asserts the mechanism by which spirit or energy vibrates and resonates your physical body back into balance and health.

Such figures, transformed by fluctuating frequencies, shift and change according to vibrational entrainment to the central nodes of the sound waves impacting them. What created the variations in the shapes of these designs was "the phase differential, or the angle between the two curves," Pettersson wrote. In other words, "the way in which their rhythms or periods," and their harmonics, coincided or not determined the shape and movement of the physical structures.

Likewise, pertaining to healing once again, harmonious or discordant frequencies have been shown to produce striking differences in human tissues. Sound waves from the core of the universe, or standing LIFEWAVE, entrain your DNA and other structures for cymatic healing.

Extending this thesis further, related biosonic vibrations result in everything from your unique eye color to the shape of your toes. Sure your parents gave you your eye color. Researchers have found this DNA–protein-production mechanism only about 3% of genetic function. Alternatively, more than 90% of DNA's activity is biosonic or bioelectric. This is what causes your eye color to be recreated every instant of your life.

This also explains why sleep is so rejuvenating. Likewise, the Chinese proverb, "Sit quiet, be still, Spring comes and the grass grows green," applies. Go to sleep feeling sick, tired, and weak, and awaken refreshed and healed by vibrations sourcing from the core of the universe, our Creator's heavenly domain.

In 1967, Hans Jenny, a Swiss physician and researcher, published *The Structure and Dynamics of Waves and Vibrations*. Jenny, like Chladni two-hundred years earlier, showed what happens when various materials like water, sand, iron filings, spores, and viscous substances, were vibrated on membranes and metal plates. Shapes and patterns in motion appeared that varied from "perfectly ordered and stationary" to chaotic.

Physical health versus disease chaos similarly results from harmony versus dissonance, too much or too little, core frequency transmissions.

Pettersson acknowledged Jenny for originating the field of "cymatics" that allowed people to observe the physical results of voice, tones, and song. Jenny applied the name "cymatics" to this area of research from the Greek term "kyma," meaning "wave." Thus, cymatics could be defined as: "The study of how vibrations generate and influence physical patterns, shapes, and material moving processes," including those ongoing in your cells and tissues.

In addition, using sand and a tonoscope, Jenny "noticed that when the vowels of the ancient languages of Hebrew and Sanskrit were pronounced," vibrating sand "took the shape of the written symbols for these vowels." Modern languages, including English, failed to generate these patterns.

American researchers confirmed Jenny's findings. Stan Tenen reproduced the effects using the Hebrew alphabet. He concluded that the "sacred languages" were indeed sacred in this way. Figure 14 shows a sample of his research.

This knowledge lays the foundation for understanding creationism in the strict sense from the Creator's spoken word as detailed in the *Book of Genesis*.

Before I relay more on language, please consider Jenny's demonstrations. He provided examples of cymatic elements found throughout nature—"vibrations, oscillations, pulses, wave motions, pendulum motions, rhythmic courses of events, serial sequences, and their effects and actions." These, he concluded, affected everything including biological evolution. *The evidence convincingly demonstrated that all natural phenomena were ultimately dependent on, if not entirely determined by, the frequencies of creative vibration.*

According to Pettersson, Jenny "speculated that every cell had its own frequency, and that a number of cells with the same frequency created a new frequency which was in harmony with the original, which in its turn possibly formed an organ that also created a new frequency in harmony with the two preceding ones."

In concurrence with Müller, Jenny argued that recovery from disease states could be aided or hindered by tones. Just as modern science supports, Jenny proposed that different frequencies influenced genes, cells, and various structures in the body.

Cathie E. Guzetta summarized this science in poetry and prose. She wrote, "The forms of snowflakes and faces of flowers may take on their shape because they are responding to some sound in nature. Likewise, it is possible that crystals, plants, and human beings may be, in some way, music that has taken on visible form."

Trust, Faith, God, and Introductory Alphanumerics

In *Healing Codes for the Biological Apocalypse*, Dr. Joseph Puleo and I, relayed how mathematics, the most precise language, is "God's language" because it always speaks the truth. Through Divine guidance we learned, as Hans Jenny had observed, that the Hebrew language, as well as English backwards, held a spiritual relationship with the Creator.

Dr. Puleo took the English alphabet, from A to Z, as seen in Table 5, and numbered each letter. For example, A=1, B=2, C=3, and so on.

After this, he was instructed to take the words "TRUST," "FAITH," and "GOD," and perform a mathematical translation on them.

For "TRUST," T=20 + R=18 + U=21, + S=19, and T=20 totals 98. Then he used the ancient Pythagorean mathematics method of reducing each number to a single digit. So 9+8=17; then finally, 1+7=8.

You get the same result—"8"—when you decipher the numerical equivalent of each letter first, then add their total according to the Pythagorean skein. The same thing occurs with the words "FAITH" and "GOD."

For "FAITH," F=6, A=1, I=9, T=20, and H=8 totals 44. And 4+4=8.

For "GOD," G=7, O=15, and D=4 totals 26. And again 2+6=8.

Any way you add them according to Pythagorean mathematics the words "TRUST," "FAITH" and "GOD" always add up to 8!

Eight (8) is the sign of infinity, that is, "Yah's number." It is also the number for oxygen in the periodic table of elements. Interesting because the Hebrew name for God means "to breathe is to exist." Fascinating also because to animate

63

Table 5. Derivation of English Letter Number Code

Letter & Number	Pythagorean Skein Equivalent	Key Word Number Derivations
A 1	1	T 20–2 + 0 = 2
B 2	2	R 18–1 + 8 = 9
C 3	3	U 21–2 + 1 = 3
D 4	4	S 19–1 + 9 = 1
E 5	5	T 20–2 + 0 = 2
F 6	6	98=**8** 17=**8**
G 7	7	
H 8	8	
I 9	9	F 6–6 + 0 = 6
J 10	1 + 0 = 1	A 1–1 + 0 = 1
K 11	1 + 1 = 2	I 9–9 + 0 = 9
L 12	1 + 2 = 3	T 20–2 + 0 = 2
M 13	1 + 3 = 4	H 8–8 + 0 = 8
N 14	1 + 4 = 5	44=**8** 26=**8**
O 15	1 + 5 = 6	
P 16	1 + 6 = 7	G 7–7 + 0 = 7
Q 17	1 + 7 = 8	O 15–1 + 5 = 6
R 18	1 + 8 = 9	D 4–4 + 0 = 4
S 19	1 + 9 = 10	26=**8** 17=**8**
T 20	2 + 0 = 2	
U 21	2 + 1 = 3	
V 22	2 + 2 = 4	The number 8
W 23	2 + 3 = 5	represents
X 24	2 + 4 = 6	Divinity & infinity.
Y 25	2 + 5 = 7	9 represents
Z 26	2 + 6 = 8	completion

Table shows the English alphabet and its equivalent numbers. Two or more digit numbers are reduced to single digit numbers to employ the Pythagorean skein and determine the mathematical "truth." Notice that numbers one through nine repeat; and the number 8, the universal sign for "infinity," is also the total for "Trust," "Faith" and "God." The number nine (9) represents completion.

Table 6. Column Showing Multiples of Eights (8)

Multiple of Eights	Reverse Alphabet		Alphabet w/ Numbers		Sum of Two Alphabet #s
1 X 8 = 0 8	8	Z	A	1	9
2 X 8 = 1 6	7	Y	B	2	9
3 X 8 = 2 4	6	X	C	3	9
4 X 8 = 3 2	5	W	D	4	9
5 X 8 = 4 0	4	V	E	5	9
6 X 8 = 4 8	3	U	F	6	9
7 X 8 = 5 6	2	T	G	7	9
8 X 8 = 6 4	1	S	H	8	9
9 X 8 = 7 2	9	R	I	9	9
1 0 X 8 = 8 0	8	Q	J	1	9
1 1 X 8 = 8 8	7	P	K	2	9
1 2 X 8 = 9 6	6	O	L	3	9
1 3 X 8 = 1 0 4	5	N	M	4	9
1 4 X 8 = 1 1 2	4	M	N	5	9
1 5 X 8 = 1 2 0	3	L	O	6	9
1 6 X 8 = 1 2 8	2	K	P	7	9
1 7 X 8 = 1 3 6	1	J	Q	8	9
1 8 X 8 = 1 4 4	9	I	R	9	9
1 9 X 8 = 1 5 2	8	H	S	1	9
2 0 X 8 = 1 6 0	7	G	T	2	9
2 1 X 8 = 1 6 8	6	F	U	3	9
2 2 X 8 = 1 7 6	5	E	V	4	9
2 3 X 8 = 1 8 4	4	D	W	5	9
2 4 X 8 = 1 9 2	3	C	X	6	9
2 5 X 8 = 2 0 0	2	B	Y	7	9
2 6 X 8 = 2 0 8	1	A	Z	8	9

Column of multiples of eights (8) deciphered according to the Pythagorean skein in which all integers are reduced to single digits using addition of each digit in the whole number. Example: 208=2+0+8=10; then 10=1+0=1. This number is associated with the letter A. When A=1 is added to the reverse alphabet letter Z=8, the sum is 9. The number nine (9) implies completion and results everytime the forward and backward English alphanumerics (i.e., letter-numbers) are added together.

Adam, humanity's first born, the Creator is said to have "breathed the breath of life into him." That is, element 8 carries the core energy for the miracle of life.

Once again, at the core of the grand standing gravitational wave, or universal LIFEWAVE, is the 528Hz and 639Hz frequencies which resolve to 6 and 9. These tones are "Mi," for miracles, and "Fa," for family. Brought together, these numbers create the symbol 69 for "yin" and "yang," male and female energy; the grand polarity of the universe. Combined further, as shown in Figure 3, the symbol yields the figure 8, the infinity sign—Yah's number once again. (In Times Roman font, this symbol is that of the "hurricane"—the powerful spiraling force of nature.)

The miracle number 6 starts at the top and spirals down, like DNA, to rejoin the creative stroke below. Likewise, the number 9, for completion, spirals up from below to rejoin itself above in the circle of life.

These, along with many other revelations, convinced me that language and life is based on the sacred geometry of mathematics, and encoded with electromagnetic frequencies of sound that, as Jenny concluded, relayed spiritual messages between people, and between people and Yah as well.

"Ultimately," as Dr. Puleo concluded, "You can't take mathematics, or even science, out of God, or God out of science, because that leaves you with only half the picture."[17]

Alphanumerics, the Holy Spirit, & Language Power

Knowing there was something sacred about the number eight (8), and knowing, according to the Bible, Yah always multiplies or divides and never adds numbers, Dr. Puleo deciphered all multiples of eights reduced to their Pythagorean single digit integer beginning with 1 X 8 = 8; 2 X 8 = 16 where 1 + 6 = 7; 3 X 8 = 24 where 2 + 4 = 6; and so on as seen in Table 6. He then realized the multiples of 8 produced a numerical countdown pattern—8, 7, 6, 5, 4, 3, 2, 1, 9, 8, 7, 6, 5, 4, 3, 2, 1, 9, 8, 7, 6, 5, 4, 3, 2, 1 which corresponded to the alphanumerics of the English language *backwards*!

More incredibly, as shown in the table, if you sum the alphanumeric equivalents of the English alphabet forwards added to backwards, the Pythagorean integer that always results is nine (9)—the number associated with "completion."

As mentioned, number 9 symbolizes spiritual evolution moving up from earth to the wholeness of Heaven and therein rejoining our Creator "in the Circle of Life." That is completion!

Now if there is something sacred about the English language, why is it *backwards*?

In all likelihood, the German-descended Anglo-Saxon, and later Norman, ruling elite developed this backwards (spiritually reversed) English language. They mathematically compromised Hebrew sometime between 500 to 1,000 years after the Crucifixion, shortly before historical accounts give rise to the Knights Templar. Obviously, the code is based on Pythagorean mystery school mathematics—the creative spiritual technology believed to have been acquired by the Templars during their military occupation of the Temple Mount in Jerusalem. Like the Levi priests that encoded the verse numbers in the *Book of Numbers* with the original musical scale, the old English language archetects encoded the same Pythagorean mathematics into the English language apparently due to its relevance to spiritual matters and energetic creationism. The esoteric truth about this action has remained hidden until this account, for two possible reasons: 1) The powerful knowledge of creative language was hidden in an effort manipulate and disempower the unwitting masses and keep people spiritually deprived and physically dependant—virtually enslaved—to the dictators of the modern world; and/or 2) by Divine plan, the English speaking world required a maturation period prior to engaging this revelation and potential emancipation. In either case, the English language engineers, with certain royal and secret society influence, "confused the tongues" as the Creator had done to punish egocentrists in the *Book of Genesis*. To date, the masses have remain enslaved by spiritual and metaphysical ignorance, and thereby distanced from creative intelligence and spiritual sovereignty if not shared divinity.

So that this sacred secreted knowledge would never be lost, and so only a privileged few—a global oligarchy or ruling elite—would remain privy to this empowerment, this language code remained hidden in the Bible.

The initial revelation about the alphanumeric Hebrew–English reversal was relayed in *Healing Codes for the Biological Apocalypse*.[17] Indeed, it relates to the story in the Bible that discusses the confusion of languages in Babylon. The "Tower of Babel" story begins in Genesis 11:1. It reads, "Now the whole world had one language and a common speech." Using the common speech, language, and sounds, empowered people who followed *Yah's Word* were blessed and nurtured. Soon, however, they became self-centered Godless pagans. They creatively built a "tower" that reached into the heavens. "But the Lord came down to see the city and the tower that the men were building. The Lord said, 'If as one people speaking the same language [they] have begun to do this, then nothing they plan to do will be impossible for them.'" (See Genesis 11:5-6.) So God decided to act decisively, creating the model that would later be used by the Anglo-Saxon/English ruling elite in their attempt to control the world through lan-

Figure 14. Cymatics of Hebrew Sounds Forming Their Respective Letter Shapes

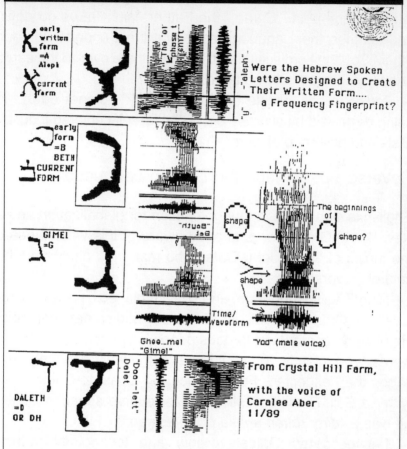

Were the Hebrew Spoken Letters Designed to Create Their Written Form....
a Frequency Fingerprint?

The beginnings of shape?

From Crystal Hill Farm, with the voice of Caralee Aber 11/89

A Frequency Picture Alphabet..

... Speaking of the Shape of Sound.

11/89

In observing these spectral pictures of our alphabet...

Diagram shows "frequency fingerprints" of the first four Hebrew alphabet letters recorded by frequency registration graphing equipment. "Frequency Picture Alphabet" graphs of letters Aleph, Beth, Gimel, and Daleth are shown formed from their spoken tones. Source: S. Tenen and D. Winter in "A Personal Journey into the Truth," A self-published workbook, 1998, by J. Puleo.

69

guage, colonialism, economic fascism, militarism, and petro-chemical/pharmaceutical dependence.

In Genesis 11:7, God moved to destroy the earliest Baby-lonian rulers' plan. "Come," the Father said, "let us go down and confuse their language so they will not understand each other." So, "the Lord scattered them from there over all the earth, and they stopped building the city."

Today, in my humble opinion, the "city"—planet earth—is being destroyed by similarly disrespectful self-centered industri-alists and political profiteers.

Reverse Speech and the English Language

English is clearly the language chosen for globalization and a New World Order. I was already aware of this when I heard the thesis of David John Oates, the man who pioneered the field of "reverse speech."

"The English language, and speech played backwards, re-lays truths from the soul," Dr. Oates claimed on national radio. He played segments of famous people's speeches, but back-wards. Very clearly you could hear completely different mes-sages than expected. For instance, on Coast-to-Coast radio with Art Bell, President Bill Clinton's reverse speech claimed he was a *"dirty rotten snake oil salesman."*

I investigated Oates's theory and technology further. Based on this study, and the information relayed above, I con-cluded that English is mathematically related to Hebrew, but electromagnetically, bioacoustically, and spiritually *back-wards!* This, I concluded, is one of many reasons humanity is morally regressing rather than socially progressing.

English, you know, reads from left to right while Hebrew reads from right to left. Why? Ultimately, because spiritual warfare can be broadly affected by reversing the frequencies and polarity of speech and this creative dynamic of language and brain function.

Science shows the right hemisphere of your brain is more active spiritually and intuitively. Rational reasoning is processed more by your left hemisphere. Language is similarly divided. In adult brains, language typically empoys the left brain, while your right hemisphere engages creative and artistic domains. You might say your left brain speaks, and your right brain sings. Thus, the left brain serves more scientists; the right side blesses more artists. The two sides are like mirror images of one another, or polar opposites, which partly explains the view that "men are from Mars, women are from Venus."

Digressing for a moment on this important topic, relationships are based on faith and trust. These needs are most commonly and heavily challenge by language or communication breakdowns. In fact, your most troubling relationships best serve to reflect your own 'deficiency needs'—that which you haven't owned or integrated into your own personality. Stressful relationships best bring these to the surface for your maturation, clearing, and healing. In fact, through the mathematical matrix graphed in Figure 10, you attract precisely what you resist, or reap what you sow, electromagnetically.

Returning to the topic of reverse speech, children are increasingly being diagnosed with dyslexia, reversing their letters and numbers. This is occurring more commonly with the advancing Spiritual Renaissance. These children are naturally more intuitive and creative, expressing their right brains. Yet, parents and teachers provide them with pathological labels, "they need 'special education,'" insisting they learn our backwards, spiritually-stifling, English language. Ironically, this is called a 'civilized society,' with officials pledging "no child left behind."

Worst of all, when the direction of reading words and articulating them in speech is reversed, as it is now with the sacred Hebrew language transformed alphanumerically into Babylonian English, it literally violates your spiritual connection and optimal brain function.

Healing Language in the Holy Kingdom

Through the introduction of foreign tongues, we sustained the loss of the edified (educated and enlightened) congregation or community. Thereafter, fear and hate replaced love and communion. Later, English dialects developed. Instead of speaking sacred and spiritually uplifting "tongues," such as Hebrew and Sanskrit, lesser languages developed without tones that relayed essential spiritual frequencies. That is, harmonic sounds that delivered health and vitality through the Holy Spirit have been mostly missing from modern languages. Thus, increasingly, human beings were distanced from each other, as humanity was from our Creator.

Clearly, there is strength in unity. Apparently, we are not destined to be enslaved forever by unloving egomaniacal earthly rulers. This is why the healing language in the Heavenly Kingdom is Love and music. The creative language of unity—Love from the heart—is spreading so widely and rapidly today, it is like a grand tsunami baptizing all humanity.

As it was in ancient Babylon, so it is now. God breaks his security contract—His covenant of personal protection—and withdraws from those who do not speak the "divine language," reflecting faith, trust, Love and humility.

Of course, you may recall, in the beginning there was only Yah, His word, and the creative fluid—water. Nothing else existed according to Genesis 1:1, when "the Spirit of Yah moved

upon the face of the water." Many scientists and Bible schol-
ars believe that the Creator, His word and water are, therefore, inseparable—linked universally by the Holy Spirit. For all
practical purposes, these parts are the same. And since we
are creations of this word, this frequency vibration on water,
we are one with our Creator-in-Love. Indeed, Love is the force,
the music, that unites us all.

Dr. Sir Peter Guy Manners, among the world's leading experts in cymatics, argued that the electromagnetic frequencies of sound and words project powerful messages and
forces throughout the universe's creative ether that clearly alter matter's form and function. The vibration of Love is a great
example because most people are familiar with the adage
"LOVE HEALS." At this unique time in history, our Creator
wishes you to understand this power in the Divine language of
the heart.

Words are communicative and attractive forces used to
create, destroy, and produce miracles for good and evil
people alike. This is why Yahshua counseled in Matthew
12:34-36:

> "For out of the overflow of the heart the mouth speaks. The
> good man brings good things out of the good stored up in
> him, and the evil man brings evil things out of the evil stored
> up in him. But I tell you that men will have to give account on
> the day of judgment for every careless word they have spo-
> ken. For by your words you will be acquitted, and by your
> words you will be condemned."

The frequency flow in every case is from the heart. Evil,
angry, fearful, and/or guilty people's hearts are burdened and
blocked. Their loving heart chakra energies are blocked. Others' hearts have evolved to freely transmit the Creator's loving
language and holy harmonies.

Regarding your condemning words, your "judgement" is immediate and cumulative. Besides the affect your harsh cause in other people that hear you speak, your condemnations resonate within you as soon as you speak them. They create or destroy your water structures as shown in Figure 6. They enable or disable your DNA as shown in Figure 5. They heal or make you sick!

Restorative Wisdom, Righteous Restoration and Free Speech

Our Creator wants you to speak the more spiritually sensitive language of Love now. To harmonize Divinely with the rest of humanity, our common language must be based on mutual respect, trust, and Love. These chosen conditions bind humanity in Divine commonality so that together we may be empowered as a unified intelligence community. These uplifting revelations about creative language leave devil-doers, whose hearts are closed to such wisdom, to their own undoing.

What does it mean to walk righteously and joyfully "on earth as it is in Heaven?" Righteousness means "right-standing(ness)." It implies your steps are firmly placed on sacred spiritual ground, "on earth as it is in heaven." It means your actions are right in line with the Creator's (mathematical) laws. You enter into this Holy Kingdom simply by following these laws—or mathematical *Word*. When you live and travel precisely in this dimension, then your every step is Divinely ordered as Proverbs 20:24 and Jeremiah 10:23 attests. Thus, you walk in health, prosperity, joy, and grace according to His covenant (i.e., protection and security contract) which is described in Genesis 26:5 and Matthew 24:45-47. This is how the Messiah was able to walk on water.

Table 7. Stan Tenen/Meru Foundation's Operational Meaning of Hebrew Letters Numerologically Matched to the Original Solfeggio Scale of Sound Frequencies

According to Stan Tenen's "MATRIX OF MEANING," the sacred Hebrew language demonstrates the operational meaning of each letter in relationship to the other letters, based on a natural model of unity, what he calls, "the hypersphere." This is technically the same as Müller's standing gravitational wave theory, or Haramein's "Grand Unification Theory." "At the abstract level," Tenen wrote, "the 27-letters correspond to the basic pointing directions" in the hyperdimensional [mathematical matrix of] space. Applying Tenen's functional meanings to the six (6) note ancient Solfeggio frequencies found in the Book of Numbers, and Rodin's mathematical matrix, yields the following metaphysical messages or spiritual encryptions:

3	9	6		6	3	9
Shine	Upright	Multiply		Expanse	Abstract	Bind
4	1	7		7	4	1
Itself	Will	Project		On & on	Divide	from All
5	2	8		8	5	2
Possess	Hold	Enclose		Puff Out	Connect	Break Open

Source: Tenen S. Meru Foundation. http://www.meru.org/letteressays/letterindex.html#MatrixOvrview

The metaphysics master Yahshua stood so solidly on these principles of the mathematically-fractal cosmos,[13] by his faith and trust he Divinely communed with, and thus transcended, gravity and the material world.

King David, in his prayer to Yah in Psalm 17:4-5, beautifully summarized this—your opportunity and spiritual connection to language. Relative to the importance of words, Divinely-ordered steps, and subsequent heavenly rewards, he prayed, "You probed my heart, you visited me at night, and you assayed me without finding evil thoughts that should not pass my lips. As for what others do, by words from your lips I have kept myself from the ways of the violent; my steps hold steadily to your paths, my feet do not slip."

Similarly, James 3:2-11 reads:

> [T]he tongue is a tiny part of the body, yet it boasts great things. See how a little fire sets a whole forest ablaze! . . . The tongue is so placed in our body that it defiles every part of it, setting ablaze the whole of our life . . . With it we bless Adonai, the Father; and with it we curse people, who were made in the image of God. Out of the same mouth come blessing and cursing! Brothers, it isn't right for things to be this way. A spring doesn't send both fresh and bitter water from the same opening, does it?

Your Divine spirit is screaming to be purely heard—to be acknowledged, loved, and loving. If you long to celebrate health, happiness, and prosperity through your relationships and Divine connection, then consistently speak as the Messiah modeled. The grand resolution and global restoration is at hand. The Creator, the Son, their Holy Spirit, and Angelic Army are working in unison to rectify earthy deceptions, reverse damages, and celebrate with you the prophesied thousand years of world peace. Prepare your heart and watch your words because they prime your preparation.

Spiritual Ignorance and God's Language

Many people can't get this simple profound truth about your spoken words creating your life, heaven or hell. It can be difficult to comprehend this mathematical matrix upon which the Holy Spirit flows with creative and restorative potential. This power is accessed by faith, trust, and prayer, and is readily available at this time and most critical for planetary renewal and miraculous healings.

Apostle Paul advised the Messianic Jewish community about their Spiritual ignorance in this regard. His words challenge all of us to live the language of Divine spiritual fulfillment. In 1 Corinthians 2:6-16. He wrote:

> Yet there is a wisdom that we are speaking to those who are mature enough for it. But it is not the wisdom of this world, or of this world's leaders, who are in the process of passing away. On the contrary, we are communicating a secret wisdom from God which has been hidden until now which, before history began, God had decreed would bring us glory. Not one of this world's leaders has understood it; because if they had, they would not have executed the Lord from whom this glory flows. But, as the *Tanakh* says,
>
> > "No eye has seen, no ear has heard
> > and no one's heart has imaged
> > all the things that God has prepared
> > for those who love him."
>
> It is to us, however, that God has revealed these things. How? Through the Spirit. For the Spirit probes all things, even the most profound depths of God. For who knows the inner workings of a person except the person's own spirit inside him? So too no one knows the inner workings of God except God's Spirit. Now we have not received the spirit of the world but the Spirit of God, so that we might understand the things God has so freely given us. These are the things we are talking about when we avoid the manner of speaking that human wisdom would dictate and instead use a manner of speaking taught by the Spirit, by which we explain things of the Spirit to people who have the Spirit. Now the natural man does not receive the things from the Spirit of God — to him they are nonsense! Moreover, he is unable to grasp them . . . But the person who has the Spirit can evaluate everything . . . .
>
> As for me, brothers, I couldn't talk to you as spiritual people but as worldly people, as babies, so far as experience with the Messiah is concerned. I gave you milk, not solid food, be-

cause you were not yet ready for it. But you aren't ready for it now either! For you are still worldly! Isn't it obvious from all the jealousy and quarrelling among you that you are worldly and living by merely human standards? . . .

Your lips are bioacoustic and electromagnetic spiritually-creative instruments. This is vitally important information for personal and world health. If you use a manner of speaking "taught by the Spirit," then you will "receive the things from the Spirit of God."

Speech, tones, sounds, music, and the vibratory essence of the Creator's Spirit, are all math-based technologies that rely on wave frequencies. Spiritually mature and intelligent people, enabled to act on this wisdom, are naturally empowered to heal, be whole, and helpful. Hold this knowledge and power dearly to solve the primary problem plaguing humanity since the "Tower of Babel"—communication. The word itself says it all. It instructs you to "commune." Bond with others and the Creator in the Spirit of Love.

Simply put, to recapture what was lost, you simply need to echo the Creator's language. Have your lips move to express truth, love, faith, praise, and harmony. Then you will earn your right to "walk on water."

Chapter Eight:
Walk On Water

Now that you know the mathematical and linguistic basis of the universe, how sound frequencies travel to bless or curse your reality; resulting in the crystallization of matter, good or bad, the next questions to consider are, "How do you manifest optimally, as a divine creation, operating in this matrix of energy?" and, "Can you actually 'walk on water'?" This chapter details the first answer. With this recognition, the second answer is obvious. You already "Walk on Water!"

Advanced Protein Crystallization Facility (APCF)

As shown in Figure 13, evaporating ice particles and gaseous water forms have been photographed in space. Solid evidence shows that water abounds throughout the universe. National Aeronautic and Space Administration (NASA) investigators have concluded this water is the matter from which cosmic bodies crystallize.[29]

Now additional NASA scientists are busy investigating why and how crystals form on earth different from in space. When crystals return from space, astronauts noticed they change. Using various analytical equipment, precision X-ray beams, synchrotron radiation, sophisticated detectors, and data-processing equipment, researchers determined the internal arrangement of atoms in space crystals differ from similar atomic arrangements on earth. Maps of these changes have been developed by scientists claiming to expand our understanding of biological processes occurring at the smallest molecular level.[29]

Figure 15. Crystals of Protein and Viruses Grown By Scientists in Micro-gravity Space

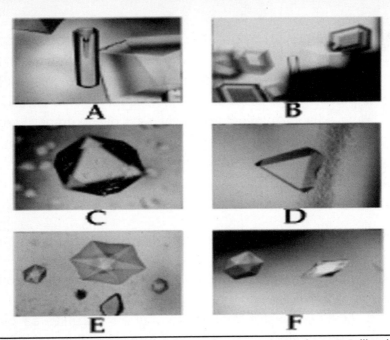

Notice the sacred geometry of these viruses and proteins crystallized in space water solutions magnified 40x. These NASA photos reinforce the knowledge that water is the universal creative medium. Matter crystallizes and flows in water. This is due to gravitational forces and frequencies of sound moving atomic and molecular matter along paths of least resistance. Focal points for matter's movement are Müller's In(6) logarithmic node set (i.e., the 3s, 6s and 9s). All atomic and molecular matter naturally flows into sacred geometric forms in these nodal regions of the grand LIFEWAVE. These reflect the harmonics in mathematics and Divinity. These forms of physical matter commune into larger bodies along these same paths of least resistance. These larger masses shown, viruses in the microcosm, reflect the macrocosm of creative frequencies which generate planets and galaxies.

This research also shows NASA scientists creating extraterrestrial viruses, with genetically modified atoms. These "alien" pathogens are being brought back to earth's labs for disease research—a grossly irresponsible industry threatening myriad species, including humans, with extinction. Outbreak risks, as you have likely heard, are very real. Photos from: http://liftoff.msfc.nasa.gov/Shuttle/ms/overview/apcf.html#3.

NASA investigator, Dr. Volker Erdmann, from the Free University of Berlin, studied "Crystallization of Engineered 5S rRNA Molecules." These molecules of ribonucleic acid (RNA) are related to DNA and largely responsible for protein synthesis in your body. They interact with the protein synthesis machinery of every cell and are "essential for the biological activity of ribosomes." From space experiments using small changes in gravity, "the crystallization of biological macromolecules" was observed to change depending on the amount of gravitational force applied to the growing crystals.

Principle investigator Dr. Gottfried Wagner, at the University of Giessen, Germany, studied a mechanism fundamental to life. A bacterial pigment (i.e., bacteriorhodopsin) was observed to "convert light energy to voltages" in the membranes of certain germs called "photoenergetic microorganisms." These bacteria are chemically and genetically distinct from other microbes and higher living organisms, but similar mechanisms are used to convert light energy to energy for growth and development throughout the plant and animal kingdoms.

For the APCF's Life and Microgravity Sciences Mission, Dr. Alexander McPherson, from the University of California, Riverside, studied growing varieties of virus crystals. The growth techniques studied employed a water medium with varying precipitants. Precipitant concentrations and most importantly, pHs, were varied. The acidity versus alkalinity of the crystal growth medium, that is, the hydroelectric polarity of the aqueous environment was central to the rate and size of crystal growth.

Figure 15, photos from this mission, shows crystals of proteins and viruses grown by "liquid/liquid diffusion" during NASA's program. Both crystals of protein pictured in A and B differ from crystals grown in conventional earth laboratories. "Photos C and D picture two samples of the unusually large cubic crystals of satellite tobacco mosaic virus, which are more than 30 times the size of similar virus crystals grown on Earth. The background of microcrystals seen in photo C is believed to have appeared after re-entry from space. Photos E and F show crystals of turnip yellow mosaic virus that display the unique multifaceted forms that have been observed only in these microgravity-grown crystals."[2]

What does all of this have to do with walking on water?

This research should convince you that you already "walk on water," and that you are an energetic crystallization of Love vibrations. Recall from Figure 3 the core frequencies of the universal LIFEWAVE being 528Hz and 639Hz—resonating miraculous Love and social communion. These central sounds inspire your biology, spirituality and Divine destiny. In scientific terms: 1) your spiralled proteins form from crystallizations occurring in the aqueous gel of body cells controlled by energetic mechanisms including gravitational forces, pH, and water electrolytes; and 2) the primary physical components of your body, that is, water and protein, are both heavily affected by the force of gravity, especially the standing gravitational wave.[26]

It is within this space/time mathematical musical matrix that you, as a Divine being, literally *walk on water*.

The Physical Crystallization Paradigm

As demonstrated by Müller's data in Figure 2 and Tables 3 and 4, the material universe entrains to the creative and energetic dynamics of the standing gravitational wave. Physical manifestation or materialization specifically occurs only at certain node points, as previously mentioned, reflecting the 3-6-9 matrix of forth dimensional (i.e., spiritual) mathematics. You, likewise, crystallize into physical form and energetically manifest in this space/time matrix through your LIFEWAVE synchronized DNA and spiralled-protein bioresonating body.

Your cells' electrodynamics also depend on this integrated resonating composite of cell organelle held in a crystalline cytoskeleton protein matrix based on central LIFEWAVE frequencies. With this biospiritual network, you are virtually "hardwired" to the center of the universe.[3] Thus, your cell organelle and membrane structures are in instantaneous communication with all parts of yourself and the cosmos. Your instinctive intuitive field reinforces this merging within the space/time continuum of Divine totality.[2,3]

According to LIFEWAVE™, LLC science director, Steve Haltiwanger, the fact that your body's "liquid crystal cytoskeletal proteins also possess semiconducting properties allows them to transfer charges (current) from the cell membrane to the internal structures like DNA and the mitochondria" from whence physiologic and metabolic energy flows. "The cytoskeleton of cells in a sense hardwires all of the components of the cell into a solid-state biological computer."[3] The central computer and primary universal operating station, is the mathematically and hydrosonically-constructed twin toroidal energy matrix of the grand Oneness.

Müller brilliantly detailed the mathematical basis of this space/time physicality, which is also the fundamental basis for the efficacy of a revolutionary nanotechnology known as LIFEWAVE™ patches. This "human software," simply composed of bioresonating water, amino acids, and sugars, activates body physiology much like drugs, but without the harmful side effects common among pharmaceuticals and chemicals. The future of healthcare is likely to be significantly advanced by this revolutionary science. This nanotechnology uniquely integrates the power of hydrosonically-affected energy responsible for the crystallization and function of matter.

Thus, we stand on the threshold of a complete paradigm shift in healthcare with developing nanotechnologies that honor spirituality and the quantum dynamics of bioenergy.

Now, the next two sections are necessarily technical. They are provided to support further research and developments in this field. Nontechnical and lay readers can skip ahead if desired.

Technical Features of the "Life Force"

Technically, "The wavelength of standing density waves in logarithmic space," Müller wrote, "are 2-3k, i.e., 6, 18, 54, 162 and 486 units of the natural logarithm. Half a wavelength, therefore, corresponds to 3, 9, 27, 81, and 243. These are relative scales [as in music] of 1,3 and 3,9 and 11.7 and 35.2 and 105.5 orders of magnitude. Exactly in these intervals, node points occur. . . . In the scope of these scales [as with harmonic resonance wave transference] communication between two adjacent node points can occur." Life precipitates, as does all matter in myriad forms, including the periodic table elements, centered upon these nodes."[16]

To understand why I say your biological geometry flows energetically following paths of least resistance to commune into your sacred physical form, read on.

Müller explained the utility and technicality of node points in universal design:

"The ability to modulate a standing wave is confined to its node points, because it is only in the immediate proximity of the node points that energy can be fed into or taken from a standing wave. If it is a standing wave in linear space, the node points are simply locations in which it is possible to connect an external oscillatory process [like physical crystallization, cymatic materialization, or Love frequency harmonization and amplification]."[16]

In other words, if you want to gain or give Divine energy, then node frequency physics is critical. You've heard the saying "Love begets Love," or "The Love you take is equal to the Love you make." Now you know why: it is only through Love that you can tap the awesome power of the universe. This is because the universe's central node resonates Love, and vibrates synchronously in harmony with the 528Hz frequency. You must give it to get it!

Node points of a standing wave in logarithmic space, however, are particular scales which have different frequencies assigned to them. In order to calculate these frequencies it is necessary to acquaint oneself with the mathematical foundations of Global-Scaling Theory. . . .

Müller continued, "The world of scales is nothing else but the logarithmic line of numbers known to mathematics at least since the time of Napier (1600). What is new, however, is the fundamental recognition that the number line has a harmonic structure the cause of which is the standing pressure wave [i.e., the grand LIFEWAVE].

"The reason for this logarithmic scale invariance is the existence of a standing density wave on the logarithmic number line, the node points of this density wave acting as number attractors. This is where prime numbers will "accumulate" and form composite numbers, i.e., non-primes such as the 7 non-primes from 401 to 409. Hence, a "prime number gap" will occur in this place.

"Precisely where non-primes (i.e., prime clusters) occur on the logarithmic number line, matter concentrates on the logarithmic line of measures. This isn't magic, it is simply a consequence of the fact that scales are logarithms, i.e., "just" numbers.

"So the logarithmic line of scales is nothing else but the logarithmic number line. And because the standing pressure wave is a property of the logarithmic number line, it determines the frequency of distribution of matter on all physically-calibrated logarithmic lines—the line of ratios of size, that of masses, of frequencies, of temperatures, velocities, etc. . . . The distance between adjacent node points is 3 units of the natural logarithm. Thus, it is easy to calculate all nodal values Xn by the simple formula $Xn = Y\text{-}exp(n)$ (Y being a natural standard measure, n=0, +/-3, +/-6, +/-9, . . .)

"Frequency values of node points are e.g., 5HZ (n=54), 101Hz (n=51), n032 Hz (n=48), 40,8kHz (n=45), 820 kHz (n=42), 16,5 MHz (n=39), 330,6 MHz (n=36) etc. The frequency ranges around 5Hz, 100Hz, 2kHz etc. are predestined for energy transmission in finite media. This is also where the carrier frequencies for information transmission in logarithmic space are located. Frequencies that occur near a node point are not just very common in nature but are used also in technological applications."[16]

These revelations provide a mathematical context in which our Creator's language becomes manifest and your physical precipitation and natural healing results. It helps us comprehend the electrodynamics of biocosmology, including the sacred geometry and protein crystallography of our universe, your body included. It decrees the scaler music by which space/time is resonated to become manifest in the grand LIFEWAVE of Divine design. Most importantly it focuses research and development on technologies for personal and planetary healing consistent with Divinity versus satanic sorcery. From this knowledge, taping the greatest force of free energy becomes realizable. Applying this knowledge for health and welfare promises the greatest technical advancements in history.

DNA and Bioholography:
Nervous System Projected Reality

As early as the mid 1970s, bioholography experts Iona and Alan Miller, whose works are featured in *DNA: Pirates of the Sacred Spiral*, proposed that a "biohologram" best explains the spiritual incarnation of a human being. They suggested this biohologram is "projected" by certain brain centers in your body, including the main one in your heart, depending on "standing and moving electromagnetic wave patterns at different frequencies of the spectrum in order to effect different biochemical transformations." They suggested various frequencies, from low range (radio waves) all the way up the spectrum into visible light and beyond, are involved in your nervous system's electrogenetic bioholography.[30]

In 1973, Miller and Webb emphasized the importance of sound waves, and music in this bioacoustic-driven, DNA/nervous-system-mediated, bioholographic projection. Your form of cymatic materialization, they wrote, "employs sound waves to create a movement on a surface that is used as the basis for creation of an optical hologram."[30]

Essentially, they advised, your chromosomes first resonate from, and then react to, *sound wave patterns emanating from objects in space*. Electrogenetic processes then convert these sound wave patterns into wave patterns of light that reconstruct the shape of that object in your mind and experience. Thus, you have a transformation taking place "between two levels of vibration, two media as it were, preserving a pattern in space."[30]

Illustrating the metaphysics of electrogenetics in bioholography, the Millers examined your liver for example. They wrote that the special function of your liver cells "is created by the influence of the projection of the liver pattern on [your] DNA [from your brains and nervous system] in the cells in the area where the liver is created."

The fuel for these bioholographic operations come from the sun and energized cosmos.[2]

According to early work by Iona Miller, "photons from the sun excite electrons here on earth; this high energy state is transformed into high energy phosphate bonds by the process of photosynthesis; the release of the energy stored in these bonds is the fuel of life; electrons are transferred between molecules in a downward cascade fashion to lower energy states; this action produces the electric current that produces the motion that we call life."[30]

"We are more fundamentally electromagnetic rather than chemical beings," the Millers reiterated. The void state, 'cosmic zero,' is the primal matrix and proportionately our most fundamental reality.

In essence, we emerge from pre-geometrically structured nothingness, and DNA is the projector of that field which sets up the stress gradients (i.e., Müller's node points) in the vacuum or 'quantum foam' (synchronized and harmonized with Müller's standing gravitational wave) to initiate that process of embryonic holography or holy projection of biospiritual creation.[30]

Your DNA projects your psychophysical self; then, likewise, your different brain centers and nervous system "mathematically construct objective reality by interpreting frequencies that are ultimately projections from another dimension [i.e., the 3s, 6s, and 9s domain]—a deeper order of existence that is beyond both space and time. . . ." Each one of your brains, according to Miller et al., is "a hologram enfolded in a holographic universe,"[30]

Origin of Life & Consciousness

Researchers have determined that at the instant a woman ovulates, there is a quantifiable shift in her electromagnetic fields. The follicular membrane bursts and an electromagnetically potentiated egg descends through the energetically alerted fallopian tube. Fertilization is also an energetic (i.e., spiritual) process. The sperm is negative with respect to the positively charged egg. When these yin (6) and yang (9) forces unite, the membrane around the egg becomes hyperpolarized. Thus, other sperm are excluded from this intimate, spiritually-driven, union. At this instant, the bioacoustic/electromagnetic human entity begins life with all the programming necessary to fulfill its destiny.

"The biohologram begins to function at conception and ceases only at death," the Millers advanced. "The DNA at the center of each cell creates the multicellular creature hologram.... The biohologram projected by the embryonic nervous system forms a three-dimensional pattern of resonant structures. These include points, lines, and planes that electromagnetically behave as the acoustic waves—the 'material waves of the drumhead'—acting as field guides to flowing matter and energy."[30]

"This process of 'reading and writing' the very matter of our being manifests from the genome's associative holographic memory in conjunction with its quantum nonlocality, the Millers concluded. "Rapid transmission of genetic information and gene-expression unite the organism as a holistic entity embedded in the larger [environmental/universal] Whole."

Relatedly, mystics have often called the sacred, all pervasive, creative sourcing sound, "logos" or word, the "Audible Life Stream."[30] Holy persons said that the light and sound are one. Thus, this holographic concept, the beginning of life and consciousness, might alternatively be called your Divine essence. It is the part of you that speaks of the great Oneness.

"God created man in His image." DNA, the miniature image of the grand LIFEWAVE, creates the bioholographic dynamics from which your creationistic energy fields crystallize your matter. Pribram (in 1991) likened this to a neural holographic process of creating life wherein images are reconstructed when their bioacoustic and associated electromagnetic representations, in the form of distributed mathematical data within neurologic information systems, are appropriately engaged.[30,31]

This entire bioholographic thesis is now firmly supported by recent revelations in space/time physics and Pythagorean mathematics.[2, 16, 25]

On Fractals and Disease

"The word *fractal* comes from the Latin *fractus*, which means broken or fragmented. Fractals delineate a whole new way of thinking about structure and form—even forms of dis-ease and healing processes, which organically root in the body and psyche" and are creatively inclined to be expressed fractally in bioenergetic systems.[30, 32]

Like holograms, if you magnify fractals multiple times to expose greater details in each part of the whole, hidden details emerge from their infinitely embedded structures. However, "the same self-similar patterns repeat, over and over, no matter what level you care to examine. You look closer and closer and still see the same form," the Millers explained.[30,]

Figure 16. Computer Generated Fractal Art[32]

Fractal art helps explain how matter manifests according to mathematical laws and formulas governing physicality, universal integrity, and Divine creativity. Thousands of renderings such as this have been generated by computers during the past decade simply based on mathematical equations processed by software. (See: Reference 23, Berkowitz J. *Fractal Cosmos*.)

"As above, so below!" The same Solfeggio frequencies in the grand standing LIFEWAVE, are reproduced in every strand of DNA and grain of sand. Thus, the Creator's core self is infinitely reiterated. This Divine cloning produces a wealth of mini-structures emerging from simplicity.[30]

Swinney (1999) clarified this profound technical thesis as follows:

At the most fundamental level of your individual being, . . . you must also operate by holographic principles. . . . Your internal perception of this reality is itself a hologram in your brain. It is the means of perception that gives the universe its apparent forms and solidity. It is also this holographic perception that influences the dynamics of your brain's and your body's chemistry, your self-hologram. In this perceptual hologram resides the fundamental basis of your structure and your sense of self and external environment, including your health and illness in both your physiological and psychological being. Your disease structures are incorporated within it. It is here, at this level of your being where fundamental healing and physical-psychic restructuring occur. This hologram is what I have termed the primal existential sensory self-image or existential hologram. . .Your sense of self is a holographic, existential, multisensory image."[30]

Translating this technical knowledge into practice, consider your first trip to the doctor. The first time you got sick, a parent or guardian probably said something like, "Oh! We need a doctor to get you well." This helped establish a belief system upon which the medical industry is based.

The concept that you require medical care to heal is generally, if not completely, untrue. The lie is damning to self-healing. Each intelligent cell in your body carries this dishonest imprint, or disempowering memory, until you reprogram yourself with the truth known in your heart.

You are far more powerful than others, especially "medical deities," might like you to believe. If you never deprogram your mind from false limiting beliefs, your bioholographic projection of self, and healing, depends on, in this case, pharmaceutical prostitutes. Your physical salvation then depends on a generally deceptive and deadly enterprise rather than on your Divinely-directed intent.

With this knowledge you might regain an enlightened appreciation of yourself. This is why I recommended earlier that you can recruit your cells, each of which contains the genetics of Divine intelligence, to recreate themselves, and you in the process, in the perfect image of our Creator.

Integrate these new understandings of bioholographic projection and self-actualization to secure optimal health. Redesign yourself in the image of Yah to fulfill your Divine destiny.

In this regard, Figure 16 shows computer generated fractal art. This creative rendering forms from a simple mathematical formula.[23] Varying formulas slightly results in vast differences in artistic expression. Pictures resembling cosmic creations form. These include colorful planets and spiraled galaxies, recognizable mountains, trees, and other life forms. They all fractally project onto paper. If this is creative computer art, imagine the artistic creative potential within your Divinely-designed "biocomputer." The knowledge herein provides the fundamentals for the development and design of your perfect life. From physical manifestation through cellular crystallizations, you hold the awesome power to alter history by expressing perfection and Divine harmony.

Seriously consider the artistic genius behind your human, and this universal, technology. The grand LIFEWAVE forms the Creator's canvas.

Now you have reason to believe, and should assume, this canvas is your canvas. You are, after all, a fractal image of the Creator's holographic projector. You have crystallized perfectly within the grand LIFEWAVE. You are composed of packets of creative sound and energized light flowing in a vast sea of liquid energetic potential. Your creative potential, therefore, using this knowledge, is vast. Your power is universal. What will you choose to create with this knowledge? What path will you take or where will you choose to walk? In duality, or unity?

It has been said that original sin—the point of separation between Creator and created; what psychologists call ego-based duality—began with identification with limitation: human limitations in knowledge versus superhuman-Divine potentiation. Henceforth, limitation, fear, doubt, and "scarcity consciousness" substituted for faith and trust in your preferred original reality of abundant creativity in unity with nature and Creator. Can you free yourself now from this optional illusion? Will you choose responsibly to cocreate abundance versus dissonance with nature and its universal essence . . . Love?

Walking in Love gives meaning to life. It is the interpretation and creative expression you bring to this walk, your unique path of service, that gives life meaning.

Walking in Love brings you in perfect step, Divinely synchronized and harmonized with the 528Hz (Miracle 6) frequency and the 639Hz (Family 9) unity at the heart of the universal symphony. This is more fulfilling than a walk on water. The space for this Divine exercise is called the "Kingdom of Heaven." Seeking it first produces everything else, including joy, vitality, longevity, and prosperity.

Chapter Nine:
Conclusions

In a book entitled *Food of the Gods,* by ethnobotanist Terence McKenna, historic trends and novel events were analyzed mathematically according to an interesting Time Wave Theory. Examining mathematical relationships inherent in the I-Ching's sixty-four hexagrams, this algorithm, when displayed as a wave and overlaid onto historical time, charted what McKenna called history's "the ebb and flow."

That is, McKenna's Time Wave predicted periods of great novelty in innovation, transformation, or planetary crisis. His Time Wave appeared to "correspond with surprising accuracy with such events as planet-wide mass-extinctions of species, cometary impacts, mankind's development and implementation of certain technologies, great social upheavals, and times of aesthetic renaissance. . . . The frightening thing about the Time Wave, or the exciting thing, depending on your point of view, is that, if it is correct in predicting past historical periods of novelty, then it follows that it applies to the near future. And according to the Wave, on December 21, 2012, a period of maximum tolerable novelty will be reached, or surpassed, and mankind can expect an exponential increase on par with our original apprehension of language and proto-civilization."[34]

McKenna asserted that this is not simply a *social* transformation, nor a political dispensation, but a hard fact of crisis in mathematics and physics itself. People, per se, he proposed, are not causing this, and "we're not responsible for it. We're just being pulled along by something on the scale of an earthquake. And that it affects physical law. . . . A modified hard position would be that it's something in the human collective personality that is seeking to express itself through fusion of

Figure 17. McKenna's Time Wave Theory Diagrams[34]

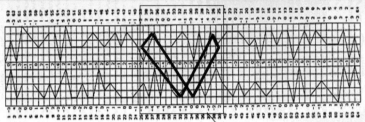

Is McKenna's "Time Wave Theory" consistent with the mathematics and physics of Müller's Standing Gravitational Wave Theory, Rodin's Math, Harramein's Grand Unification Theory, and/or the theory of hydrocreationism or "intelligent design" advanced in this book?" Very likely.

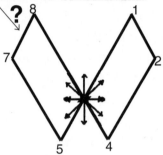

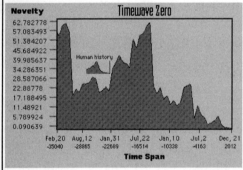

With the leftside graph, McKenna argued "human history, from the building of the Great Pyramid in 2790 BC until 2012 AD, is contrasted with the length of time during which human beings have been using fire and perhaps language. . . .

His diagram to the right purportedly demonstrated the power of McKenna's theory to anticipate historical events. "Every major episode of great novelty since the birth of the Prophet Mohammed appears in its proportional importance here." McKenna wrote. "It is clear that with striking accuracy the Time-wave correctly predicts the ebb and

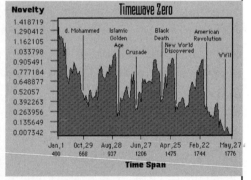

flow of history." From: McKenna T. The Time Wave and History. For more information see: http://www.levity.com/eschaton/twzdemo.html

all the individuals into some kind of cyber-organic matrix whose intent lies in the collective unconscious of the species, and we don't know what that is. . . .

"And then [there is] the soft position," McKenna added. "There's a group of people on the Internet called 'singularists.' And they are complete tech heads, engineers, not an iota of psychedelic or spiritual manna in them. But they take all these engineering curves—curves of energy release, curves of speed, curves of population, curves of information densifica-tion—and reach exactly the same conclusion, that some time between 2010 and 2020, life becomes unrecognizable. We apparently possess starships, can build nano sites, can down-load ourselves into circuitry, can completely control our ge-netic expression, remain immortal, transform into other species, on and on and on, just based on the programs in place in R&D at the corporate-state level. . . .

"[A] lot of people are anxious [about this]. This [theory and evidence] causes anxiety," McKenna counseled. "It needn't. It isn't a bad thing. It's scary because the future was postponed for so long that now the breaking of the logjam is going to look like Armageddon. But it isn't Armageddon. What lies beyond all this I think, is the first authentic human civilization. These are the pre-pre-times.

"You know Gandhi was once asked what he thought of Western Civilization and he said "It sounds like a veddy good idea."

As shown in Figure 17, McKenna's theory may correlate well with the intelligence advanced in this book. If the consen-sus of contributors to this book's creationistic thesis is correct, the artistic genius behind both human and universal evolution legally operates mathematically. Heaven is the grand math-ematical matrix formed for our Creator's, and your cocreative, canvas.

Entropy and Momentum

My wife and I had an enduring difference of opinion. Jackie, a far more organized person than I, harped incessantly about my seeming inability to put things away; in their "proper" place(s). My "mess" tolerance was far greater than hers, and I justified my position scientifically. I asserted the definition of *entropy*. "Things tend to move towards chaos," I defended. "It's a waste of time to organize in a home with children that make messes. Like the universal tendency toward entropy, disorganization and randomness is a certainty. Get used to it!"

Since the time of this writing, I've changed my mind.

Created in 1875, around the time modern science was established, the term *entropy*, and its history, is important in this discussion of mathematical certainty and universal integrity. Examples of modern definitions of "entropy" include: "1. *Symbol* S for a closed thermodynamic system, a quantitative measure of the amount of thermal energy not available to do work; 2. A measure of the disorder or randomness in a closed system; 3. A measure of the loss of information in a transmitted message; 4. The tendency for all matter and energy in the universe to evolve toward a state of inert uniformity; 5. Inevitable and steady deterioration of a system or society."[35]

Technical discussions of entropy aside, following this research, it seemed odd to me that *order* or *organization* was generally unrecognized as the natural tendency of matter in our evolving world. "Inevitable steady deterioration" of our social system seemed inconsistent with Haramein's Grand Unification Theory and Rodin's perfect mathematical matrix. The tendency of things in our universe to disburse randomly, and become disorganized with time, is an obvious contradiction when there is mathematical certainty and Divine organization in reality. I could only conclude that chaos is allowed, even encouraged, in the context of teaching us valuable lessons regarding an overriding ordered existence, and the wisdom in bringing order to chaos. This was certainly true in my family with three children, a nagging wife, and a stubborn messy husband. Here's the lesson:

Have you ever tried and failed to stop a heavy object moving with insurmountable force and momentum? It was an exercise in futility. Jackie's forceful redirection effectively persuaded each of us to learn "tidyness." The children and I were forced to give in, despite discussions of entropy. This story about family, orderliness, force, and momentum, is a lesson best learned by those who oppose Love in this age of reconciliation.

The heart and weight of the universe is now flowing more forcefully than ever to the beat of its love and unification vibrations. The "Miraculous Loving Family" is being mathematically selected—called from dormancy by this universal symphony. Love, is the core vibration being transmitted to facilitate the Spiritual Renaissance. This is a Divine calling and destiny for humanity.

Diving into this cresting wave is the easiest, most intelligent choice. LOVE is the path of least resistance. As we stand at the crossroads of spiritual reconciliation versus organic annihilation, walking in love assures survival of those most fit to heed this direction.

Follow Your Fully Opened Heart

The scientific revelations herein speak of a central connection between your heart, which is your loving brain, and your bio-holographic projection. Every cell, in fact, mirrors the Creator's mathematical majesty and genetic imagery.

Material crystallization, physical precipitation, and biospiritual evolution depends mainly on the frequency vibrations and flow periods within the Heavenly Kingdom from which the grand LIFEWAVE flows as shown in Figures 2 and 3. Like every wave, this one has periods of peaks and troughs with different energetic qualities per phase of its cycle. The movement of creative sound frequencies within this eternal wave, flowing throughout the universe's aqueous ether, expresses the harmonic or disharmonic variations affecting space/time and the material world. The central part of the wave today is cresting globally with Love's affinity.

This wave moves with gigantic force. Mere mortals cannot resist it and survive their genetic program.

The power of human technologies pale by comparison to this Divine invention. At every moment, the LIFEWAVE's vibrations profoundly impact life. Human psychosocial behaviors, physical health, and spirituality are all affected. By the law of entrainment, the smallest human body, mostly made of water, must entrain with this universal body of water or cease by its own dissonance.

As McKenna's data attests, history must, likewise, reflect the frequency dynamics of the grand LIFEWAVE. This orderly power forcefully entrains changes within the frequencies of people's hearts, minds, and bodies. Every cell's DNA vibrates according to this supreme set of signals. These supersonics— their confluence or interference—heavily affects population. Mass mediated political and economic trends must yield to these greater unseen forces. This grand unifying theory helps explain how and why during various times in history tyrants and spiritual renaissances came and went.

Noticeably, over the past few decades, people worldwide have been awakening with enhanced spirituality and increased sensitivity to inexplicable synchronicities occurring in their lives. This is symptomatic of this expression of Divinely-directed predestined power. The paradigm shift, the transformation into spiritual hyper-drive, is occurring.

At this same time, while hastening the general acquisition of spiritual qualities and sensitivities throughout humanity, there seems to be an equally intense purging of negativity. This is reflected, for instance, in unprecedented high rates of divorce, new plagues, sociocultural unrest, increasing rates of crime, aggression, political discontent, and general malaise. A new supreme order shall emerge from this politically orchestrated or simply mismanaged chaos. As the volume is amplified in the central frequency range of 528Hz and 639Hz, the major frequencies for Love, miracles, and family, positive outcomes are destined to emerge globally.

The mathematical revelations contained herein also help explain astrology, numerology, and other metaphysical fields of interest. Personal biases of unenlightened practitioners aside, accurate prognostications simply reflect the mathematical order and Divine balance reflected in the cosmos. The Bible's counsel against placing faith and trust in practitioners in these fields relates to the frailties and inconsistencies of being human versus Divine. Supreme intelligence is reflected in these arts and sciences, but not necessarily in a practitioners skills.

Those with "closed hearts" unable to consciously choose LOVE in this Age of Enlightenment will simply implode from their own dissonance. They will suffer heart failure from their own hateful, fearful, and threatened lives.

The Creationistic Approach to Healing"

Remedies for diseases, based on these extraordinary revelations in space/time science giving rise to math-based technologies involving sound and light energies, are increasingly, and more rapidly, coming of age. These biospiritual technologies, like the first LIFEWAVE™ patches and 3E stickers, use resonance frequencies for modulating physiologic processes and metabolic reactions. For health and healing, the foregoing knowledge offers new hope and direction for those interested in physical salvation and spiritual evolution beyond religious and academic doctrines.[2,3] Healing is simply explained by this Divine design and the physics of frequency mathematics.

This has nothing to do with human or religious doctrines. The world's greatest natural healer, Yahshua, taught, "The traditions of men make the Word to no avail." In other words, mental constructs such as disease labels and foreboding prognostications generally prohibit heartfelt faith and trust in the awesome power of Divine design and restoration. This scientific knowledge is scripturally certified.

There is a constant, underlying, eternal LIFEWAVE of energy fundamental to physical reality and miraculous healing. This driving life force attunes the harmonic elements of the microcosm to the macrocosm, the microscopic structures to the cosmic energy matrix. It creates unity with the Kingdom of Heaven being near (right here and now) with nothing missing nor broken herein. Spontaneous healing results by entrainment and communion with this grand matrix versus dissonant individuality.[2] This commonality represents our evolutionary destiny.

In this regard, there is great news to report on many fronts. For example, the 3E™—Evolutionary Energy Enhancer technology integrates the above knowledge in support of the consciousness revolution and Spiritual Renaissance that heavily engages water. At the time of this writing, the 3E™ is being pilot studied around the world. One investigation, on the Big Island of Hawaii considers and applies the Pacific Ocean as a Love frequency resonance amplifier. Here the ocean receives a human contribution based upon sacred wisdom to effect loving transformation (through hydro-creationism) for spiritual evolution and planetary salvation. Modulating this effort's energy is the Breath of the Earth™—volcanically heated steam from the rushing Kilauea lava flow. All of this is being used to transmit Love—Dr. Emoto's 'Message from Water,' with Divine thanks, into the South Pacific to facilitate the Spiritual Renaissance.[21]

By no accident, a huge natural heart-shaped hill protrudes from Mauna Kea's eastern slope. It greets visitors enroute to the world's most esteemed deep space observatories.

This setting, the magnificent Hawaiian holyland, is the perfect place for creationistic research and spiritual development. Beginning from the ocean floor, this is, after all, earth's highest mountain, reaching farthest from any sea into space. It, therefore, receives the most *light* from billions of galactic suns and stars. The world's best telescopes and astronomical experts are stationed here in the *heart of the world's largest body of water* to unravel the mysteries of hydrocreationism. Through analyses of sound and light emissions, they seek to discover the origin of life and the cosmos. Supplied by governmental grants and corporate contracts they search outward posing questions. In the stillness of the mountain's silence the best ones turn inward for answers.

The growing secret and scientific consensus is that the Hawaiian Kahunas are right (*Kahuna* is a Hawaiian word to mean Precious One, The Provider, or The Keeper of the Sa-

Figure 18. Spiraling Galaxy Photographed by NASA[36]

The above photograph was taken by NASA's Hubble telescope of the Barred Galaxy NGC 1300. Details here pale by comparison with images from larger newer telescopes stationed on Mauna Kea. Notice the 69-like bilateral spinning polarity of the galaxy cluster as compared with similar structures in Figure 3. This characteristic is commonly seen in space photographs. It reflects the positive and negative polarities associated with the mathematics and gravitational physics advanced earlier. This characteristic is also apparent in the photo on the right of a new cell being born. This is mitotic cell division in a rat kangaroo epithelial kidney cell captured with fluorescent microscopy. Can you see any similarities between the microscopic and macrocosmic phenomena?[36]

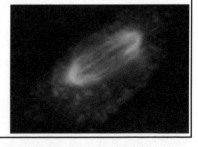

cred Principle): *the end of the universe begins right here*. The summit of this sacred place is believed by Kahunas to be the Divine umbilical cord to all creation—the birthplace of the cosmos.

On this sacred summit, spiraling galaxies of light dating back billions of years, radiating and spinning like DNA in cellular space, is observed nightly. (See Figure 18.) The origin of everything, leading scientists now posit, is animated similarly,

Conclusions

mathematically, and gravitationally. Space is filled with energized water. Its waves and force fields reflect intelligent design. Life's inexplicable synchronicities evidence spiritual
certainty.

Where else on Earth would you expect such a reasonable
Love labor to be effective in recreating and entraining ourselves and our planet, through water, in the image of our Creator?

Your contributions to help facilitate this work are invited
and greatly appreciated.

In *DNA: Pirates of the Sacred Spiral* (Tetrahedron Publishing Group; 1-888-508-4787), I scientifically reviewed your
body's bioenergetic structures and inherent vibrational
mechanisms. This book features the subtle bioacoustic and
electromagnetic properties of biological systems, genetic expression, and fractal manifestations.[21] The book explains how
and why life is engaged in cybernetic and metabolic self-regu-
lation within the universal energy field or spiritual domain.[2] If
you enjoy learning on this subject, this technical publication
provides rich background in biospirituality and electromedicine.

Western religions attest to the regulatory influence of the
Holy Spirit and Power-of-Love. Eastern theologies call this the
Universal Life Force or "chi." In Hindu traditions, "prana," the
Breath-of-Life, is physically sustaining. Common to all spiri-
tual orientations is the creative aqueous medium, water.

Water, containing the elements hydrogen and oxygen, is
the creative juice of the universe. Herein, oxidation/reduction
reactions, high-energy electron transfers, and material crystallizations occur. Through anthropology and various theologies, similar phenomena are said to underlie life and health
from the microscopic to the macrocosmic domains.[2]

The revelations advanced herein are unifying for the
world's people. Everyone, everywhere, can rejoice in this commonality—you are a water vessel and Holy Spirit-filled temple.
How you use this information and revelation to celebrate unity
and fulfill Divine destiny is up to you.

Summary and Prognosis

Suddenly, it seems, the physical and metaphysical worlds and sciences have merged. From their evolutionary attraction comes a creative, restorative, and novel vision of ourselves and the universe. This holistic utilitarian view illuminates some of history's best kept secrets. Fundamental mysteries of the universe, creationism, and humanity's roles herein have been solved. These revelations involve biophysics, biophysiology, biocosmology, electrogenetics, protein crystallography, sacred geometry, structured water science, cymatics, and more. The creative mechanics and even meaning of life are linked to ancient mystery-school Pythagorean mathematics, standing wave theory, musicology, and more. Multidisciplinary studies advancing knowledge from these fields are opening revelatory and revolutionary doors to a healthier future.

Those who effectively manipulate, coerce, enslave, and kill to feed greed, financial empires, Machiavellian geopolitical schemes, and omnicide, are being displaced in this mathematically-predestined paradigm shift. The transformation, and eventual elimination, of this rude energy blockage is naturally occurring as positive spiritual capacities supersede all physical liabilities.[2]

This alternative unifying healing paradigm has been present all along. Shifting to this paradigm has awaited scientific and theological maturity, or advanced consciousness. Increasingly, people are stepping up to the tasks required to assimilate and apply this knowledge.

The fact that nearly a third of experimental subjects in all drug trials experience natural healing solely by faith in placebo should cause pause in considering the psycho-spiritual dynamics underlying physical reality and the natural healing arts and sciences. The evidence herein proves the intimate connections between individuals and the creative cosmic realm.

Conclusions

This reality check implies that most disease results from, aside from radiation and chemical toxicity, psychosocial stressors including nocebos. You think you are sick, or may get sick, express related math-based memories, and manifest your inner image of illness for your bioholographic projection. At minimum, psycho-energetic or psycho-spiritual cofactors are vitally important in disease prevention and natural healing.

It is not impossible to walk on water when you have been doing this all along. The universe is filled with water. Reality emerges exclusively from this hydrosphere. Your Oneness with the universe and others in it unfolds in this aqueous creative medium. H_2O is the most precious common superconductor and energy carrier in the cosmos. Love is the central harmonic signal. This frequency, and entire system, operates by atonement (or entrainment) to harmonically engage and express the In(6) or Mi(6) nodes of the standing gravitational wave. These factors dictate miraculous physical manifestation and/or required destruction in keeping with homeostatic balance, mathematical laws, or the rules of universal order in the Kingdom of Heaven. Everything, including people and governments, must abide by this Divine plan to thrive or prematurely perish.

Obviously, keeping the peace, or law enforcement, in this Divinely-ordered most powerful domain relies simply on the (karmic) force of entrainment with the standing gravitational wave against which all actions, harmonic or dissonant resonances, are measured. These are the fundamental parameters by which technologies for personal and global healing must abide to optimally perform. The alternative is enslavement to something less spiritually empowered and, therefore, physically more lethal and incapacitating.

The grand LIFEWAVE is available now for surfing eternally to the shores of Divine destiny. It is my hope that you will be inspired by this knowledge, abide by the aforementioned laws, and as a result, experience the full measure of responsibility and opportunity to serve humanity in this revolutionary age of science, technology, and psycho-spiritual evolution.

Finally, a word of **warning**. As this knowledge becomes more widely known, as dissemination of this information hastens along with human consciousness, the Spiritual Renaissance will unfold mathematically, exponentially, more rapidly. It is, therefore, imperative that you rapidly prepare yourself, your heartfelt intent, and universal mind for the forthcoming social, economic, emotional, and spiritual changes destined to unfold in less than a decade.

As noted in *Healing Codes for the Biological Apocalypse*, the sound frequency interval from 528Hz—the center of your heart and the universal Love vibration—and 741Hz, the "So" tone (defined in *Webster's Dictionary* as "Solve the pollution" or the "Solve the problem") is known in music as the 'devil's tone.' It has an offensive sound quality, and it may be the principle harmonic, augmented 4th, for wielding destructive power.

Naturally, those who fail to adequately prepare themselves, and who remain behaviorally dissonant with hearts closed to the growing Love vibration, are at risk. By fear and greed, many will succumb to the destructive resonance of cosmic justice.

Devildoers will thus be susceptible to their own destruction. Those who project dissonance, the Creator's enemies, or Love's adversaries, will be destroyed by their own choice. *Take heed that you are not among them.*

The Prince of Peace was able to *Walk on Water*. His reason was to inspire you to *Walk in Love*.

About the author

Dr. Leonard G. Horowitz is an internationally known authority in the overlapping fields of public health, behavioral science, emerging diseases, and natural healing. Dr. Horowitz received his doctorate from Tufts University School of Dental Medicine in 1977. There, as a student and faculty member, he taught general and dental histology, and graduated with honors and  a fellowship award in behavioral science at the University of Rochester. He later earned a Master of Public Health degree from Harvard University focused on media persuasion technologies, and a Master of Arts degree in health education/counseling psychology from Beacon College, all before joining the research faculty at Harvard School of Dental Medicine to study psychosocial factors in oral health and disease prevention. For more than a quarter century he has directed the nonprofit educational corporation that evolved into Tetrahedron, LLC (http://www.tetrahedron.org).

Dr. Horowitz's earlier books include the American bestseller *Emerging Viruses: AIDS & Ebola—Nature, Accident or Intentional?* Now considered a medical classic, this publication earned Dr. Horowitz the "Author of the Year Award" from the World Natural Health Organization in 1999, the same year he released *Healing Codes for the Biological Apocalypse* which permanently expanded the field of musicology.

Dr. Horowitz's second best-seller was *Healing Celebrations: Miraculous Recoveries Through Ancient Scripture, Natural Medicine and Modern Science* (2000). It provides practical information and advice for self healing.

In June, 2001, three months before the terrorist attacks of 9/11, Dr. Horowitz released the prophetically-titled critically-acclaimed book, *Death in the Air: Globalism, Terrorism and Toxic Warfare*. This book summarized the leading global industrialists' efforts to enslave humanity through toxicity and petrochemical/pharmaceutical malfeasance.

His 2004 book, *DNA: Pirates of the Sacred Spiral,* reviewed the science of electrogenetics that speaks to humanity's fundamental spirituality.

Aside from an active speaking schedule, Dr. Horowitz oversees the Steam Vent Inn & Health Retreat on the Big Island of Hawaii, where one of the world's most powerful natural healing resources—volcanically-heated steam—is being used to help explain Divinity to humanity.

For more information about Dr. Horowitz visit his official website at http://www.drlenhorowitz.com, attend his weekly conference calls through http://www.healthyworlddistributing.com, or visit the "Creator's Rainbow Spa" online at: http://www.steamventspa.com.

Other Dr. Horowitz affiliated websites:

http://www.healthyworlddistributing.com
http://www.3epower.us;
http://www.originofAIDS.com;
http://www.C-CURE.net;
http://www.healingcelebrations.com, and
http://www.tetrahedron.org

References

1) King C. *BIOCOSMOLOGY*. Department of Mathematics, University of Auckland, New Zealand, 2003; Link to: http://www.dhushara.com/book/bchtm/biocos.htm)

2) Horowitz L. *DNA: Pirates of the Sacred Spiral*. Sandpoint, ID; Tetrahedron Publishing Group, 2004.

3) Haltiwanger S. The science behind LIFEWAVE™ technology patches. Atlanta, GA: LIFEWAVE™, LLC, 2005. Link to: http://www.lifewave.com/pdf/haltiwanger_24p_paper.pdf)

4) Mendelsohn R. *Confessions of a Medical Heretic*. New York: Warner Books, 1980.

5) Horowitz L. *Emerging Viruses: AIDS & Ebola—Nature, Accident or Intentional?* Rockport, MA: Tetrahedron Press, 1996.

6) Horowitz L. *Death in the Air: Globalism, Terrorism and Toxic Warfare*. Sandpoint, ID: Tetrahedron Publishing Group. 2001.

7) Manning P. *Martin Bormann: Nazi in Exile*, New York: Lyle Stuart, 1981.

8) Miller MI, Christensen GE, Amit Y, Grenander U. *Mathematical Textbook of Deformable Neuroanatomies*, Proc. Nat. Acad. Sci, USA 1993;90:11944-11948

9) Chervenak F and McCullough L. Ultrasound for all: By whom and when? How often? Presented before the First World Congress On: Controversies in Obstetrics, Gynecology & Infertility. Praque, Czech Republic, 1999. (Link to: http://www.obgyn.net/displayarticle.asp? page=/firstcontroversies/prague1999chervenak-mccullough2)

10) Toga AW and Thompson P. An Introduction to Brain Warping. In: *Brain Warping*. Arthur W. Toga, Editor. Los Angeles: Academic Press, 1998.

11) Becker RO and Selden G. *The Body Electric*. New York: William Morrow & Co., 1987.

12) Anonymous. *Blast It! The Ultimate Rife Researcher & User Manual*. KeelyNet, 2002.(Link to: http://www.keelynet.com/products/blastit.htm).

13) Emoto M. *The Message from Water* vol. 3 Love Thyself. Tokyo: IHM Research Institute, 2004

14) Keutsch FN and Saykally R J. Water clusters: Untangling the mysteries of the liquid, one molecule at a   time. Inaugural Article Chemistry *PNAS* 2001;98,19:10533-10540 (Link to: http://www.pnas.org/cgi/content/full/98/19/10533)

15) Underwood A, Whitford B, Chung J, et. al. Spirituality in America. *Newsweek*, Sept 5, 2005, pp. 46-64.

16) Müller H. *Theory of Global Scaling.* Sante Fe: NM: Institute for Space-Energy-Research, Leonard Euler, Ltd. and Global Scaling Applications, Inc., 2002.)

17) Horowitz L and Puleo J. *Healing Codes for the Biological Apocalypse.* Sandpoint, ID: Tetrahedron Publishing Group, 1999.

18) Goldman J. Holy Harmony Tuning Forks: Sacred Sounds for Modern Times. Boulder, CO: Spirit Music, 2000. Available through Healthy World Distributing, LLC, 1-888-508-4787 (www.healthyworlddistributing.com).

19) The Phi Nest. DNA: The spiral is a Golden section; the cross section is based on Phi. Lengthy analysis and discussion is available online at http://www.goldennumber.net.

20) Personal communication from Lee Lorenzen who had used this frequency to energize his C400 "Cat's Claw" clustered water formula..

21) Personal communication from David Schmidt following his mathematical investigation of 528Hz.

22) The simple technology known as the Evolutionary Energy Enhancer (3E™) is discussed at: http://www.3epower.us.

23) Berkowitz J. *Fractal Cosmos: The Art of Mathematical Design.* Oakland, CA: Dharma Enterprises, 1994

24) K Liu, JD Cruzan and RJ Saykally. Water Clusters. *Science* (16 Feb) 1996;271:929-931.

25) Haramein N and Rauscher EA. The origin of spin: A consideration of torque and coriolis forces in Eisnstein's field equations and Grand Unification Theory. *Special Issue of the Noetic Journal* Vol. 6 No. 1-4 June, 2005, pp. 143-162. ISSN 1528-3739.

26) Advanced Protein Crystallization Facility. Information from the U.S. Government, National Aeronautics and Space Administration (NASA) available on the Internet at: http://liftoff.msfc.nasa.gov/Shuttle/lms/overview/apcf.html#3

27) To learn more about the LIFEWAVE™ product line, or embrace the network marketing opportunity, contact the person(s) who recommended this book to you. Otherwise, go online to http://www.healthyworlddistributing.com, or call toll free 1-888-508-4787.

References

28) Horowitz LG. *Healing Celebrations: Miraculous Recoveries Through Ancient Scripture, Natural Medicine and Modern Science.* Sandpoint, ID: Tetrahedron Publishing Group, 2000

29) Staff. Cold Clouds and Water in Space. *Astrobiology Magazine.* June 4, 2001; online edition available at: Spacehttp://www.astrobio.net/news/modules.php?op=modload&name=News&file=article&sid=14.

30) Miller I. *The Holographic Paradigm and the Consciousness Restructuring Process,* Grants Pass: Mankind Research Unlimited, 1993. See also: Miller RA, Webb B, and Dickson D. A holographic concept of reality. In: *Psychoenergetic Systems,* ed. Stanley Krippner, Vol. 1, 1975, 55-62.

31) Pribram K. *Brain and Perception: Holonomy and Structure in Figural Processing.* Hilldale, NJ: Lawrence Erlbaum Associates, 1991.

32) This fractal art sources from T.C. Design, Eye on Design available on the Internet at: http://www.tcdesign.net/fractals.html

33) For information about joining the "BioSpiritual Dreamteam," or Trinity Weath Foundation call 1-888-508-4787, or write to Dr. Horowitz in care of Healthy World Distributing, LLC, 206 N. 4th Avenue, Sandpoint, ID 83864.

34) McKenna T. Interview in *Hootenanny Magazine.* Available from: http://www.hootenanny.com/hoot/4/mckenna.html.

35) Definitions of entropy from: www.thefreedictionary.com.

36) Photograph of spiraling galaxy courtesy of NASA's Hubble website. See: http://hubblesite.org/gallery/album/galaxy_collection/pr2005001a/large_web. For photomicrograph of mitosis see: Molecular Expressions website at: http://micro.magnet.fsu.edu/cells/fluorescencemitosis/.

Walk on Water

Notes

Astonishing revelations about Divine creation, with revolutionary new healing applications, this book provides startling proof of heaven on earth; the musical manifestation of the material world, and the mathematics of spirituality and Love connecting your heart, more than your head, to the center of the universe!

If your search for purpose and meaning in life is ongoing; if you've been challenged by modern stresses and strains; if political events, economic burdens, and environmental concerns trouble you; or if your health and well-being needs boosting, award-winning author declared modern-day prophet, Dr. Leonard Horowitz, provides an unparalleled peek into the Creator's technology. He unearths compelling scientific evidence of your spiritual existence, and gives practical advice for your success as a powerful co-creator.

Learn to be openhearted, optimally blessed, and Divinely directed and protected as dramatic changes are unfolding globally. This spiritually uplifting book will have you celebrating and powerfully contributing to the Spiritual Renaissance as modern life is being transformed worldwide, and people like you are doing their part in preparation for a millennium of world peace.

If you are interested in alternative medicine, metaphysics, music, simple mathematics, chanting, or praying, Dr. Horowitz relays great news. *Walk on Water* "opens doors that no man can close" regarding your spirituality, unity with Divine family, and the importance of your family and community for personal development, spiritual evolution, and planetary salvation.

continued on backcover